Libera

From a Mother To a Daughter to Restore Liberty

Volume 1

Written by Pamela J. Adams
Edited by Brent N. Adams

Copyright © 2015 by Pamela J. Adams

All rights reserved. This book or any portion thereof may not be reproduced or used in any manner whatsoever without the express written permission of the publisher except for the use of brief quotations in a book review.

Printed in the United States of America
First Printing, 2015

ISBN 9781533384980

This book is dedicated to America, both young and old. May we find and embrace the truth before it is too late.

It is also dedicated to my husband who has been my rock, my sounding board and my strength for over 23 years. Thank you for our Groovy Kind Of Love.

Lastly, I dedicate this book to my precious daughter, Trinity Grace. I started writing these letters for you. I pray you will find peace, comfort, answers and guidance in them. Your future is whatever you make it. So make it a good one.

Table Of Contents

Is Consensus Always Right?	April 24, 2014	1
"Soylent Green Is Made Out Of People!"	April 27, 2014	2
The Sounds Of A Revolution	April 28, 2014	4
Fruit Of The Forbidden Tree	May 2, 2014	6
Change The World	May 5, 2014	8
A Hero's Story	May 8, 2014	10
A Mother's Perspective	May 11, 2014	12
Hear No Evil, Speak No Evil	May 18, 2014	14
Memorial Day – Honoring The Highest Sacrifice	May 26, 2014	17
The Real Hunger Game	June 1, 2014	19
D-Day vs. Today - How Far We've Come	June 6, 2014	22
Father's Day	June 15, 2014	25
Sleeping Beauty	June 21, 2014	27
The Candy Bomber	June 24, 2014	31
The Birth of a Movement	June 29, 2014	34
Happy Independence Day	July 4, 2014	38
WWJD	July 13, 2014	42
Man On The Moon	July 20, 2014	45
America's Pale Blue Trabant	July 24, 2014	48
The Cost Of Capitalism	August 4, 2014	52
Is History Repeating Again?	August 7, 2014	55
Independence: It's In Our DNA	August 13, 2014	58
Just The Facts, Ma'am	August 20, 2014	61
Family Feud	August 27, 2014	64
The Man Who Refused To Be King	September 3, 2014	68
Never Forget	September 11, 2014	71
We Reserve The Right To Refuse Service	September 18, 2014	75
Is Justice Blind?	September 24, 2014	80
Actions Speak Louder Than Words	October 2, 2014	84
What Is Columbus Day?	October 13, 2014	89
Keeping The Faith	October 20, 2014	94
Love The One You're With	October 24, 2014	97
The Knock Heard 'Round The World	October 31, 2014	99
The Truth Shall Set You Free	November 3, 2014	103
Happy Veterans Day	November 11, 2014	108
A Tale Of Two Women	November 19, 2014	110
Thanks Be To God	November 27, 2014	113
Thanksgiving Proclamation 1777	November 27, 2014	118
Yes, Liberty, There Is A Santa Clause	December 6, 2014	120
Glass Houses	December 12, 2014	123
I Believe I Can Fly	December 17, 2014	127
The Reason For The Season	December 25, 2014	129
Quotes		132
Picture Credits		135
References		136

Is Consensus Always Right?

April 24, 2014

Dear Liberty,

In the late 1890's there were several inventors who were trying to conquer flight. All of them were using the same scientific numbers for air and lift. Why? Well, because there was a consensus that these were the numbers. After all, Otto Lilienthal was the most respected aeronautical scientist of the nineteenth century and he had developed the data on lift. In addition, John Smeaton had determined the coefficient of air pressure at .005 based on his experiments with windmills. Smeaton's Coefficient was the scientific standard for over 150 years...and wrong.

It was only after the Wright Brothers came along and challenged those respected authorities that flight became possible. The brothers conducted experiments using their own wind tunnel and discovered that the numbers being used were incorrect. But how can that be? Everyone agreed that these numbers were the data to use. Lilienthal and Smeaton were scientists, the Wrights merely bicycle builders.

How wonderful is life here that we have the ability to continue to do experiments, improve technology, and discover better, more accurate, data to tell us more about our world and everything in it.

Thank you, Orville and Wilber, for not giving in to the consensus and striving for truth rather than popularity and acceptance. This, Liberty, is why you should never settle for the argument that 'there is a consensus' or that any dissent to that consensus is ignorant, backwards, and illegitimate. Strive to be right, strive to be true, strive to be accurate.

That's my 2 cents.

Love,
Mom

"Soylent Green Is Made Out Of People!"

April 27, 2014

Dear Liberty,

Phil Hartman made this line popular in the 1990's on Saturday Night Live while mocking a 1973 movie in which the world's food source turns out to be made from people. In 1999, "The Matrix" went further by turning humans into batteries to power artificial intelligence. Both of these stories where set in the distant future with far-fetched concepts that could never happen.

2014. We have just discovered that not only has a hospital in the UK been using aborted babies as fuel for 13 years, but also a British Columbia company has been sending human tissue waste, including aborted babies, to Oregon for the same purpose. If the mere thought of that doesn't warm you, just toss another baby in the furnace.

When you remove the preciousness and value of human life from society's foundation, then is it really that far-fetched to accept that it's reasonable to slaughter your own offspring for your convenience and to use them as fuel as well?

God warned the Israelites to not worship like the pagans who sacrificed their children to the fire god, Moloch. Live babies were placed into the arms of the statue of Moloch and as the arms were raised the baby would roll into a fire burning inside the statue. The worshipers sang and played music to drown out the cries and screams of the baby being burned alive. Today those worshipers sing a new tune of "pro-choice" and "global warming".

Liberty, we are living in a time right now where people are again championing the sacrifice of their children for convenience, for birth control, and now for fuel. Those who worship the Earth, or the creation, over the creator will burn babies without regret, but decry the use of nuclear, clean coal, or natural gas.

The Bible and history have recorded the horrific rituals done to both animals and man, oftentimes for the gods to provide rain or provide for the harvest. Many would argue that we are so much more advanced and 'evolved' now. Really? How are we any different than the pagans of Biblical times? We are sacrificing our children to appease the gods of climate change.

Liberty, you will hear and see many disturbing things in your life. You will wonder how the people who preach tolerance are willing to accept such evil that we do to each other. These things are not happening because there is no God, these things are happening because we have made ourselves gods.

That's my 2 cents.

Love,
Mom

The Sounds Of A Revolution

April 28, 2014

Dear Liberty,

SPLASH! It was a splash and not gunfire that announced the beginning of the American Revolution and it was, in all respects, a peaceful resistance. After being forced to buy only British tea and then having to pay an exorbitant tax on that tea which the British did not have to pay, the colonists decided to send a strong message to the King. Though history books often portray this event as wild and out of control, the Boston Tea Party was actually quite organized. The colonists made sure to only discard the tea and no other goods so as to make their point loud and clear. No one was killed. No one was even caught. But the protest was not really about the tea, it was about the refusal to allow the colonies to self-govern. (see <u>Tyrants And Tea Parties</u>-Vol.4)

What is even more amazing is the first shot of the Revolutionary War, or War of Independence, still did not come for another 16 months. (see <u>The Shot Heard 'Round The World</u>-Vol.3) Even with this anger, even with this dissent, the colonists still were trying hard to fight for their freedom and resolve their differences with the crown not with bloodshed, but with diplomacy, petitions, and peace.

By the time the Declaration of Independence was actually penned, taxation without representation was only 1 of 18 abuses of the King. Grievances of the colonists were by far more in concert with freedom to govern and rule themselves. For years the colonists appealed again and again to have their complaints heard and addressed by the King. He answered with more laws, more harassment and more government. (see <u>Acts Of Oppression</u>-Vol.4)

"In every stage of these Oppressions We have Petitioned for Redress in the most humble terms: Our repeated Petitions have been answered only by repeated injury. A Prince, whose character is thus marked by every act which may define a Tyrant, is unfit to be the ruler of a free People." - Declaration of Independence

Liberty, it is interesting how we are once again going through a very similar struggle, but this time with our own government. Even though we now have elected representatives, many feel that once they get to Washington those representatives no longer listen to the people.

More restrictions, more laws and more taxes are placed on the people while those in authority actually remove themselves from the very regulations they write. America is once again under the stronghold of authority and that authority is refusing to listen to the people.

Just as Americans had to decide for diplomacy or violence in the beginning, and just as Americans had to decide for peaceful resistance behind Martin Luther King Jr. or violent protests under Malcolm X, Americans are deciding right now whether to fight with words or with swords. I pray that like with the colonists and with civil rights in the 1960's, the spirit of America that I love and know will again choose to fight peacefully and resist picking up arms for as long as they possibly can. When you read this in the future I pray that you will find strength and comfort and respect that your parents, along with millions of other Americans, held on to our history and to our pride and fought the good fight with love, courage, and honor.

That's my 2 cents.

Love,
Mom

Fruit Of The Forbidden Tree

May 2, 2014

Dear Liberty,

A few days ago a well-known and likable actress, Swoosie Kurtz, confessed that she had an abortion when she was young. She said it was an anguishing time in her life. As I listened to her confession I expected her to reveal her regret for that difficult decision. Instead she lamented how tough it was finding a doctor to perform an abortion. She added that she hopes we do not revert to a time when only the rich will be able to afford safe abortions. Swoosie took a debate over if it is right to slaughter a child, and made it into a debate over how convenient we should make it.

I reflected over these comments and was reminded of the gravity of man's fall into sin. In Genesis, God tells Adam and Eve to refrain from the fruit of the "tree of the knowledge of good and evil" and says they would surely die if they ate of it. Before the fall, Adam and Eve respected God's laws and obeyed them without question. As a result God blessed the couple with heaven on earth, a utopia, called the Garden of Eden. Satan, using the same trick he still uses today, asked Eve, "Did God really say that?" He convinced Eve that eating from the tree would make her as wise as God, allowing her to decide what was right and wrong. The result was not that humans became wise, it's that they began to determine for themselves what was good and evil.

God's law is constant and it is established for our good. However, society has taken all of God's commandments and flipped them upside down. As an example, if you kill an attacker you can be prosecuted for defending your life, but we are required to provide taxpayer-funded abortions. Coveting and stealing are not wrong, they are merely ways of trying to make society equal. Baring false witness and lying are perfectly fine if you do it for the common good. Fornication and adultery are not wrong, merely human weaknesses. So where are we now? Your great-grandmother use to leave her door unlocked at night. Now I carry a gun for your safety. Has society improved?

I think it's time to turn back to God.

When society starts telling you what is good and evil, it can redefine what is good and evil. Those with power and influence can start controlling what you do, what you say, and what you think by *punishing you for your "evil" actions. German society slaughtered 6 million Jews because Hitler labeled them as evil. Stalin massacred 11 million Ukrainians because they refused to conform to collectivism, which made them evil. Mao Zedong killed over 45 million of his political enemies, disobedient citizens, and workers too old to produce because such actions were evil. Your liberties can be taken away in a blink of an eye by someone who believes they are wiser than you and has placed themselves in a position to determine what is good and evil. As I stated in "<u>Soylent Green Is Made Out Of People!</u>", Liberty, it's not that there is no God, it's because we have made ourselves gods.*

Liberty, God is not a ruler, He is your Heavenly Father. You are He precious child. Think of how your Earthly father loves and adores you even when you do wrong. Because of that love he has rules, guidelines, and yes, sometimes discipline. How much more do you think your Heavenly Father loves and adores you? He gives us rules, not to limit our happiness, but to give us happiness.

That's my 2 cents.

Love,
Mom

Change The World

May 5, 2014

Dear Liberty,

There are millions of people in this world who wish to change the world. They all want to feed the hungry. They all desire to help the poor. They all stand-up for women and children who are abused. They all want to respect the earth. And they all are truly sincere about those causes.

The problem is they usually fall into one of two ideologies that unfortunately are in complete opposition to each other. Both change the world, but not quite in the same way. The first gives the individual the power to make change while the second forcibly tries to make the change for the collective, and thus, gives an elite group power. The first gives individuals liberties and the second takes them away. One holds individuals responsible for themselves while the other takes all responsibility, and freedom, away from the individual. One allows individuals to freely give, help, and touch people's lives for both now and in eternity while the other just takes from individuals and the help just barely affects another's daily struggles. For the first, change takes place constantly but is often more felt internally for both the giver and receiver than externally. To the latter, change usually needs to be seen externally for confirmation that any good was even done. More importantly, since the change was usually the result of an elite group forcibly taking the gift and distributing it to the receivers, the chance for any love, respect, or true personal change is denied the opportunity to even be allowed to occur.

It boils down to the all-inclusive statement of we want to "save the world". What does that mean? To the Christian, to save someone means their soul will be in heaven for eternity. To the non-Christian, to save someone means the time here on earth will be more bearable. In a society where we have developed an "instant results" mentality, it is easy to be enticed and now a days quite frankly bullied, into pushing for the oh so desired utopia here on Earth. Liberty, it doesn't exist. If it did, why are multi-million dollar actors overdosing on drugs while others are perfectly happy without even a TV?

Liberty, you will be seduced by your friends, by your co-workers, by politicians and by society as a whole to fall into the latter school of thought. But you need to ask yourself what good is just saving *someone's present when their eternity will be lost in hell? Are we supposed to show compassion for the hungry and the poor? Absolutely. But if we follow Christ and understand what his life, death and resurrection really mean, our hearts can do nothing else but love our neighbors as ourselves. We won't need some bureaucrat in Washington telling us they are going to take more of our money to give to someone else. We the people, through our churches and synagogues, will be doing that.*

Before acting, make sure to ask yourself, are you doing it because either you want something in return or you are being forced/bullied into doing it, or are you taking action because Christ sacrificed everything for you and the Holy Spirit has filled you with the desire to share His love with others?

That's my 2 cents.

Love,
Mom

A Hero's Story

May 8, 2014

Dear Liberty,

  Night was descending and all the soldiers around him had fallen one by one. They were picked off like targets at a carnival shooting game as the enemy sent shells whistling through the air toward the 9-man company. He steadied himself behind his machine gun and waited for the next German to dare show himself in the clearing in the trees. BOOM! A bomb explodes and sends him hurling through the air. BOOM! Another bomb explodes and returns him to the bunker he coveted for shelter. Was there help? Were there reinforcements? Would he survive?

  This was the long night of May 8, 1918, your great-grandfather, Lawrence, had in World War I that awarded him a purple heart and a silver star. Lawrence held the German forces away through the evening, by himself, until his buddies came to look for the squad in the morning and rescued him. By keeping the Germans away he held the field for the allies and prevented a full attack by the Germans.

  Out of drinking water, grandpa drank the only thing he could find, the water in the machine gun that was used to cool it. For his bravery, he received lead poisoning and nearly died. He was blown out of and back into the bunker several times which resulted in a back injury that plagued him the rest of his life. But despite all of this, even after Lawrence had to shoot a German who managed to make it up the hill, he still left the safety of his bunker to help the wounded enemy only to find he was too late.

  Liberty, this is only one of the incredible stories in your lineage of the brave, courageous, and patriotic ancestry that you have. (I will share more in future letters.) Nothing was given to your great-grandfather. In fact, everything had been taken away from him by the time he was 16. His mother died of cancer when he was 7 and his father, George, was killed 8 years later.

  George along with his two employees was going over a bridge on his thrashing machine when it fell off the bridge, pinning him against a stone wall. His middle was crushed but his only concern was that his two companions were ok and safe. "Mr. R. was accompanied by two colored men, George and William B., on the engine. When the engine went down, his assistants were thrown into the creek and miraculously *escaped serious injury. Mr. R. insisted, however, that the men who were endeavoring to extricate him should help the others before doing anything for him." (The Interior Journal – August 26, 1910)*

George had made an agreement with his neighbor that if anything happened to him, the neighbor would take care of the children. When the time came, the neighbor took everything George owned, including a town store, and left the children to fend for themselves. Lawrence found himself working on the farm of a family friend for pennies and living in meager housing for 4 years. His only chance for freedom was lying about his age and enlisting in the army.

He had his father's entrepreneurial spirit though. While in Texas chasing Pancho Villa in 1914, he did laundry for his fellow soldiers to make money. (see The Forgotten General-Vol.2) He was part of history, being assigned to the 2nd machine gun battalion in the "Big Red One" (see Duty First-Vol.4) and not only remembered seeing the Red Baron fly above them in the skies, he saw the Red Baron shot down. It is no wonder Lawrence became the most decorated WWI veteran of his town with 2 Silver Stars, a Purple Heart, a Fourragère aux couleurs de la Croix de guerre, and many victory Medals.

Several years after the war and getting married, Lawrence found himself living in the Great Depression with a wife and child. He had a job at ARMCO (American Rolling Mill Company) and would go there everyday to see if he would be able to work. The operators did their best to spread the work around so everyone got a chance to make some money. On the days Lawrence wasn't chosen, he farmed a small plot of land allowing him to feed his family. After the Depression, when work was steady, Lawrence decided to do what he could to move ahead. With only a 4th grade education, he taught himself the slide rule (no small feat if you know what a slide rule is) and educated himself enough that he could become a supervisor. No one did this for him, not even a teacher. He did this totally on his own.

Liberty, don't let anyone ever tell you that you don't have the right to speak or to have an opinion because you are "privileged". Your ancestors have put their blood, sweat, and tears into this country for your God given right to do just that. They deserve our respect, not our disdain. Know your heritage, know your rich, spiritual inheritance and never, ever be ashamed of it.

That's my 2 cents.

Love,
Mom

A Mother's Perspective

May 11, 2014

Dear Liberty,

Today is Mother's Day. I have a wonderful mother, your grandmother, who I will write to you about later because all I can think about today is how thankful I am to be your mother.

Your dad and I had been married almost 19 years with no plans of children when we found out about you. From that moment on my life has never been the same. From that moment on I had a real purpose. From that moment on I have been a mom. I can't even remember life without you.

Thank you for saying, "morning, mommy" every morning and "night, mommy, I love you," when I put you to bed. Thank you for saying "please", "thank you" and "you're welcome" and shaking pastor's hand as we leave church. Thank you for hiding behind my leg when you meet someone new and saying "goodbye, see you later" when we leave them. Thank you for giving me hugs and kisses and screaming "again, mommy" when I give you zerberts. Thank you for requesting "come here, mommy" more times than you shoo me away. Thank you for stating "one more time" five times in a row as you run around the playground to go down the slide yet again. Thank you for climbing up on grandma's piano and playing your own tune while proudly singing "Jesus", and that's your only lyric. Thank you also for belting out the words to 'Wagon Wheel' after seeing a Duck Dynasty display in the middle of the Family Christian Store.

Thank you for looking to me for guidance and thank you for forgiving me when I make mistakes. Thank you for testing your independence but still running to my arms when you need me. Thank you for giving me the chance to see the world through different eyes.

You have made me into the person I've always wanted to be. Because of you I have more compassion, more understanding, more patience, and more love than I have ever had before. You've helped me realize what's really important and what can be laughed off. Vaseline on grandpa's family rocker and butt paste all over your Fisher Price tent set come to mind. You have allowed me to have more careers and accomplishments than I could have ever achieved on my own in the business world. You make me laugh, you make me cry, you make me *smile, and you make me proud.*

Thank you for coming into my life and allowing me to be your mom.

That's my 2 cents.

Love,
Mom

Hear No Evil, Speak No Evil?

May 18, 2014

Dear Liberty,

Recently, the 15th Annual White Privilege Conference was held with 2,500 teachers, school employees, and high school students attending. During this insightful meeting several amazing statements were made, but this letter will just focus on the idea of Freedom of Speech.

One presenter, a professor, stood up in front of the group and proclaimed Obama is just a Black face in the White Privilege House. She then joked she had tenure so she feels safe to make her comments. It is understood she has the unchecked freedom of saying whatever she wants to in the classroom without any repercussions. No one can monitor her statements or her ideology, to which she was thankful.

A short time later, another presenter lamented that in America, because of our unlimited "Freedom of Speech", anyone can say anything they want no matter how hurtful it is for others. She held up as an example Germany, revealing it is illegal for Germans to talk about the Nazis. She was proud that the German leadership removed that shameful time from their history and their dialogue so no one would be inspired to repeat the violence of the National Socialist Party. Liberty, though they may be sincere, these speakers are incredibly, incredibly dangerous.

First, they say that they don't want to say anything that could hurt others or cause violence, while they daily target Christians, conservatives and any other opinion that dares not conform to their accepted "free speech" philosophy in the classroom. Furthermore they promote taking a physical stance against these people including the use of violence and even death. We are already seeing a confrontational attitude on campuses across the country, sometimes ending in physical harm.

William Ayers, member of the 1960's Weather Underground, a professor, progressive leader, and mentor to Barak Obama, believes as many as 25 million Americans will need to be eliminated if they do not re-educate themselves to give up capitalism and embrace socialism. His ideology is a modern continuation of the American progressives that gave Hitler the idea of the gas chamber. In the early 1900s California eugenicists, funded by prominent progressive institutions, promoted and carried out ethnic cleansing practices including sterilization, segregation, and openly discussed using gas chambers for group executions of undesirables. Hitler praised the work done by these American eugenicists in <u>Mein Kampf</u> and followed their example in carrying out his Jewish Holocaust. (see <u>Sanger And Eugenics And Socialism, Oh My</u> – in Volume 2)

Second, as Edmund Burke said, "Those who don't know history are destined to repeat it." Right now in Germany, where they are unwilling to discuss Nazis for fear of renewing such hatred, there is a huge resurgence of Nazism. While Germany is trying to protect its citizens from the horrors of Nazism, it is allowing history to repeat itself.

In Greece, after its recent economic collapse, a large Nazi population has emerged there as well. This group calls themselves Golden Dawn. The Golden Dawn, like the Weather Underground, is merely a resurgence of an earlier hate group. This political party has offices in both Greece and Germany, but has now spread to England, Australia, Canada and the US. The Golden Dawn has been anything but non-violent in Greece. By not educating the people about their past, the Europeans are embracing this horrific ideology rather than resisting its hate filled rhetoric.

Liberty, those of the Progressive Party in the US try to scare the American people about the Tea Party and Conservatives by describing them as Nazis. The media frequently describes the Nazi Party as a "far-right" movement, trying to link it to those that believe in individual freedom. This is a mislead by the very people wishing to take your freedom. The media is using a European view of politics, rather than an American view of politics, to describe the Nazis. (see <u>There's Nothing Right About The Alt-Right</u>) You have a cousin in Austria, who argued with me that the Nazis were politically 'right'. I argued that they are clearly a party of the 'left.' We were both correct, merely using different scales. Scales the media uses to weigh an argument in their favor.

In Europe, the left and right are defined by whether they are more communist, (European left) or more socialist (European right). The problem for the Europeans is that both schools of thought are big government institutions, they just disagree on how that big government should rule its people. America, on the other hand, defines the left and right by the extremes of full totalitarianism on the left, (communism and socialism), and complete anarchy on the right, or the absence of any government at all. The American left distance themselves from Nazism and try to demean the right wing and conservatism by calling them Nazis. The truth is, in an American context, Nazism falls well on the side of the left. The Nazi ideology goes hand in hand with the modern progressive/socialist agenda. After all, it was the National Socialist Party. In fact, Hitler got his ideas from the mentors of the same people who try to use the Nazi brand as a political tool against their conservative opponents. The differences in European and American politics are very important to understand and remember so that you do not fall into the media's trap.

The media, like modern teaching, comes from the 100+ year old progressive push to turn America into a socialist nation. "Capitalism and Christianity are the source of all our problems," is the underlying progressive thought. Hitler used a similar argument against the Jews so he could kill 6 million of them. Progressives want government to be their god and will do everything they can to make that happen. They first have to beat you into submission by taking over the language and imprisoning you by using "political correctness." They make any dissenters completely paralyzed from criticizing them and then just shove through their agendas, waiting to destroy any remaining mavericks who try to stop them. They make perfect movie bad guys. However, they make very dangerous politicians.

Liberty, if you have any politically incorrect viewpoint that someone doesn't agree with, hold firm. You do not have to give up your rights just because someone believes they can bully you into submission. Unfortunately, some people are convinced that their rights trump yours. However, their rights STOP where yours begin. Others just assume they know better than you and are justified in telling you what to think. Never be afraid to speak your mind or defend your God-given right to do it. You have the right to speak, they do not have the right not to be offended. You will be called names like racist, bigot and hater, and that your views are unacceptable. Be quick to point out that the intolerance in this situation is not coming from you. In fact, the hatred being spewed is not yours, but that of your accuser.

One last thought on Freedom of Speech. If someone who is white is preaching to you about "white privilege", do you really have to listen to them? After all, by their own admission they have been privileged their whole lives and anything they say is just meant to control you. If, on the other hand, a minority professor preaches to you about "white privilege", isn't the fact that they are in such a position of authority completely discredit their argument that whites are in control and oppressing their views? Whether a person is white or black, Freedom of Speech gives them the right to state their opinion. In this case, it's clear that some people haven't given their opinion a lot of thought.

That's my 2 cents.

Love,
Mom

Memorial Day - Honoring The Highest Sacrifice

May 26, 2014

Dear Liberty,

Remember only two defining forces have ever offered to die for you.
Jesus Christ and the American Soldier.
One died for your soul, the other for your freedom.

With indescribable selflessness the American solider puts his life on the line to win and keep the freedoms and liberties that we are privileged with every single day. You are blessed to have the blood of many of those brave servicemen flowing through your veins. One of your great-grandfathers was part of the Big Red One (see Duty First-Vol.4) in World War I (see A Hero's Story), while two others served in World War II along with several great-great uncles. You have relatives that served in the Korean, Vietnam, and Persian Gulf Wars and one of your grandfathers was even stationed behind the Iron Curtain during the Cold War. Your family has been honored with such brave patriots and fortunate that only four of those courageous men have fallen during wartime, each called home during World War II. Attacks at sea took the lives of two great-great uncles who were brothers, just 2 months apart. One was in England in the European conflict while the other was in the Pelilieu Islands in the Pacific. The Invasion of Normandy claimed one cousin while the Battle of the Bulge took another. Like so many other Americans, who have lost their lives at war, their tragic loss is the price of our freedom.

But even greater than the love, respect, and thankfulness that we have for our fallen soldiers is our reverence and gratitude for the sacrifice of our Lord and Savior, Jesus Christ. While the soldier dies for his family, his country, and his freedom, Christ died for all, giving believers freedom from sin, death, and the power of the Devil. Christ led the perfect, sinless life that we could not and took upon himself our deserved punishment. He sacrificed himself to redeem us from the curse of death. He was, in all reality, a one man army, defeating the forces of Hades single-handedly in 3 days and claiming victory for us all.

The Father of our Country, the humble, God-fearing General George Washington, understood this, demonstrating his belief in Christ every single day of his life. With an open Bible on the chair in front of him, Washington prayed for an hour on bended knees every morning and every evening. His faith and strong moral code, built on the firm foundations of God's word, guided him through the bleakest days in our country's history. May we as a country return to the same devotion and understanding of the Lord's ultimate sacrifice, knowing that the greatest battle has already been won. Even though we still struggle with the curse of sin in this world and the wars which result, by the sacrifice of Christ our salvation has already been won and our eternal salvation proclaimed. May we humbly thank God for our blessings this Memorial Day, sharing in a prayer of thanksgiving given by General Washington.

"O eternal and everlasting God, I presume to present myself this morning before thy Divine majesty, beseeching thee to accept of my humble and hearty thanks, that it hath pleased thy great goodness to keep and preserve me the night past from all the dangers poor mortals are subject to, and has given me sweet and pleasant sleep, whereby I find my body refreshed and comforted for performing the duties of this day, in which I beseech thee to defend me from all perils of body and soul.

Direct my thoughts, words and work. Wash away my sins in the immaculate blood of the lamb, and purge my heart by thy Holy Spirit, from the dross of my natural corruption, that I may with more freedom of mind and liberty of will serve thee, the ever lasting God, in righteousness and holiness this day, and all the days of my life.

Increase my faith in the sweet promises of the Gospel. Give me repentance from dead works. Pardon my wanderings, and direct my thoughts unto thyself, the God of my salvation. Teach me how to live in thy fear, labor in thy service, and ever to run in the ways of thy commandments. Make me always watchful over my heart, that neither the terrors of conscience, the loathing of holy duties, the love of sin, nor an unwillingness to depart this life, may cast me into a spiritual slumber. But daily frame me more and more into the likeness of thy son Jesus Christ, that living in thy fear, and dying in thy favor, I may in thy appointed time attain the resurrection of the just unto eternal life. Bless my family, friends & kindred unite us all in praising & glorifying thee in all our works begun, continued, and ended, when we shall come to make our last account before thee blessed Saviour, who hath taught us thus to pray, our Father."

George Washington's Prayer Book.

That's my 2 cents.

Love,
Mom

The Real Hunger Game

June 1, 2014

Dear Liberty,

Last weekend there was another tragic mass killing in California. The killer was a 22-year old college student whose father was the director of the movie Hunger Games, a story about an oppressive government that forces children to kill each other for sport. He had nice clothes, $300 sunglasses, a BMW, expensive toys, and a famous father, yet he was miserable.

Despite all the trappings of success, he felt isolated from society and held an animosity towards everyone around him. He became a self-centered loser, angry at everyone who failed to worship him. Since people failed to respect him, he had to get even. To carry out his deadly act of vengeance, he planned on using hammers, knives, guns and an SUV to fulfill his scheme of carnage, described in gory detail in his manifesto.

Despite his mental state, and both his plans and actions of using multiple weapons, the gun control soldiers started their march, hitting the spotlight right on cue. They claimed they were looking out for people's safety, while advocating taking freedoms and liberties away from citizens. They deliberately ignored his 141-page proclamation that revealed the root cause of his actions was a decline in society, not an access to guns. It is additional proof that those attempting to ban guns by claiming to do so out of concern for society is a blatant lie used to push forward their harmful agenda. While politicians blame everything from the 2nd Amendment to the Tea Party, arguing that the only solution is to remove guns from society, they refuse to truly look at the honest root of the problem - our removal and denial of God.

While reading excerpts from his manifesto it dawned on me how incredibly lost this man, and our society as a whole, is. In both his written statement and a YouTube video, this very disturbed young man confessed he was taking revenge on his classmates for refusing him. He revealed that his social life completely died when he got high-speed Internet and became obsessed with violent video games, where killing can become a high to players as addictive as any drug. He claimed they filled the void of loneliness in his life. Burning anger towards women consumed him because they denied him sex while a deep hatred for the men getting sex compelled him to violence. His self-delusional utopia placed him as supreme ruler, where he could deny women the right to choose mates and starve them in concentration camps. Yet, he still longed for a girlfriend. Though he developed one of the most unhealthy, nauseating views of women, deep down, in his own words, he revealed how much he simply wanted someone to love him.

The spate of recent mass shootings consistently shows one thing; the perpetrators are anti-social people. Most claim they are trying to fill an emptiness inside and too often they are filling that void with violent, destructive video games. Once violent games, movies, music, drugs, alcohol, or pornography turns into a steady diet, the person can't help but be influenced by what he takes in, often leading to destructive results.

At the same time we have an overwhelming push to remove God from any and all parts of our lives. We see it in the turn from God in our movies, memorials, schools, courtrooms, government, and in some cases, churches! While a small group want to blame the guns, the truth is, too many people have nothing else to hold on to. We have so devalued life with the worship of abortion and evolution that some, when they commit these atrocities, feel absolutely no remorse. Why should they? There's no eternal consequence and the person they killed was just an accident of nature anyway.

Guns have been around since the forming of this country with a very low number of deaths occurring at schools. For most of our history the shootings that did occur were acts of passion or anger and only resulted in 1 to 2 deaths. Today, we have mass killings where the suspects plan their path of destruction for weeks or months in advance, consistently revealing they want to kill as many as they can, wanting to induce as much pain as possible. What has changed? These people are hurting, searching for something in their lives to make them feel worthy. They live in a very real Hunger Games, hungering for the Bread of Life, Jesus Christ. However, rather than addressing this issue, it is easier to blame the gun. By doing so, the gun control advocates can steal your freedom without fixing the problem, an abandonment of God.

Liberty, Satan is working very hard to destroy every soul on the face of this Earth and he will use every means possible to do it. Are Christians perfect? Absolutely not. But when you study God's Word you will learn of the overwhelming love He has for you. You will know that before you were even conceived God had a plan for you. Everyone is loved by God and He desires that every soul be with Him in paradise. You will also acknowledge that we are to love others as we love ourselves. If you appreciate the preciousness of life and the value that God puts on each and every one of us, than you will know that using a deadly weapon can only be done in the defense of life. These poor souls are so lost and feel so worthless, there is no way they can view the value *in others because they see no merit in themselves. As you go through this life, continue to study and understand the Word of God. Share it with others so the voids they feel might be filled.*

There is a woman right now in Sudan who has been convicted and sentenced to die. Her crime? She's a Christian. She is married to an American and gave birth to their second child while in prison. The judge gave her several chances to spare her life if she would renounce Christ and convert to Islam, but she would not recant. That is the faith you must strive for, Liberty. Because of that faith, she is already free. She has hope. She has courage. She has love.

That's my 2 cents.

*Love,
Mom*

D-Day vs. Today - How Far We've Come

June 6, 2014

Dear Liberty,

Today is the 70th Anniversary of D-Day and a commentator on the radio made the point that today's liberals could not have fought World War II. Today's liberal is about appeasement.

This point could not have been made more dynamically than by Pres. Obama releasing the top five terrorists from Guantanamo Bay last week. The desire to appease comes from the belief that it will make peace with our enemies. They truly believe that there is absolutely no time or place for war. The problem with that viewpoint is many of the adversaries we are negotiating with don't have that same perspective. They have no problem killing to get what they want. In fact, most desire it. They are more than happy to have you lie down and give them what they want. It is seen as a sign of weakness. Contrary to progressive thinking, appeasement does not satisfy the power-hungry dictator or the jihad driven Islamic extremist. It makes them stronger, bolder, and more determined than ever to completely obliterate their appeaser.

In September of 1938, Neville Chamberlain, Prime Minister of Great Britain, was hailed as the "savior of Europe" after returning from Munich where he, France, Italy, and Germany signed an agreement to split Czechoslovakia to placate Hitler. Everyone was convinced he saved Europe from another war and brought peace to the area. He prided himself on his desire and ability to appease his foes to keep peace. Six months later Hitler took over the rest of Czechoslovakia. World War II officially began just shy of a year after the Munich Agreement when Hitler invaded Poland. (see The British Bulldog-Vol.3)

Liberty, there are people in this world who just want to destroy and control others whether it be by war or by taking your rights, freedoms, and liberties by deceit. If you do not stand for your rights, someone will come and take them. Though war should be a last option, it should never be considered completely off the table because your enemies will ultimately resort to it no matter how much you give in to them. As Saint Augustine stated, "Though defensive violence will always be a sad necessity in the eyes of men of principle, it would be still more unfortunate if wrongdoers should dominate just men."

22

D-Day is an example of the honor, integrity, resilience and endurance Americans have shown over the years. But even more important than that is the faith and reverence Americans have had for Almighty God. There was a time when Presidents, whether Democrat or Republican, would unashamedly offer prayers to God as is demonstrated in this message from Franklin D. Roosevelt on June 6, 1944 - D-Day.

"My fellow Americans, last night when I spoke with you about the fall of Rome, I knew at that moment that troops of the United States and our allies were crossing the channel in another and greater operation," Roosevelt said. "It has come to pass with success thus far. And so in this poignant hour I ask you to join with me in prayer."

Almighty God: Our sons, pride of our Nation, this day have set upon a mighty endeavor, a struggle to preserve our Republic, our religion, and our civilization, and to set free a suffering humanity.

Lead them straight and true; give strength to their arms, stoutness to their hearts, steadfastness in their faith.

They will need Thy blessings. Their road will be long and hard. For the enemy is strong. He may hurl back our forces. Success may not come with rushing speed, but we shall return again and again; and we know that by Thy grace, and by the righteousness of our cause, our sons will triumph.

They will be sore tried, by night and by day, without rest-until the victory is won. The darkness will be rent by noise and flame. Men's souls will be shaken with the violences of war.

For these men are lately drawn from the ways of peace. They fight not for the lust of conquest. They fight to end conquest. They fight to liberate. They fight to let justice arise, and tolerance and good will among all Thy people. They yearn but for the end of battle, for their return to the haven of home.

Some will never return. Embrace these, Father, and receive them, Thy heroic servants, into Thy kingdom.

And for us at home – fathers, mothers, children, wives, sisters, and brothers of brave men overseas – whose thoughts and prayers are ever with them – help us, Almighty God, to rededicate ourselves in renewed faith in Thee in this hour of great sacrifice.

Many people have urged that I call the Nation into a single day of special prayer. But because the road is long and the desire is great, I ask that our people devote themselves in a continuance of prayer. As we rise to each new day, and again when each day is spent, let words of prayer be on our lips, invoking Thy help to our efforts.

Give us strength, too – strength in our daily tasks, to redouble the contributions we make in the physical and the material support of our armed forces.

And let our hearts be stout, to wait out the long travail, to bear sorrows that may come, to impart our courage unto our sons *wheresoever they may be.*

And, O Lord, give us Faith. Give us Faith in Thee; Faith in our sons; Faith in each other; Faith in our united crusade. Let not the keenness of our spirit ever be dulled. Let not the impacts of temporary events, of temporal matters of but fleeting moment let not these deter us in our unconquerable purpose.

With Thy blessing, we shall prevail over the unholy forces of our enemy. Help us to conquer the apostles of greed and racial arrogancies. Lead us to the saving of our country, and with our sister Nations into a world unity that will spell a sure peace a peace invulnerable to the schemings of unworthy men. And a peace that will let all of men live in freedom, reaping the just rewards of their honest toil.

Thy will be done, Almighty God.
Amen."

What an amazingly humble prayer from FDR. May we find our way back to this reverence and understanding of God before we become the nation that righteous men fight against. May we not only begin to cherish our history again but may we also learn from it. May we remember that yes, we were founded and governed for a long time by people in both political parties who believed in Almighty God and turned to Him, especially in times of trouble and war, for guidance and victory for the righteous. May God hear our prayers and soften the hearts of those who have hardened them against Him. May we stop putting our faith and trust in men and government and return to the one, true King, our Heavenly Father. As He did so many times before with His people Israel, may God have compassion on His people in America, forgive us, and remit the demise that is coming our way. In Jesus Christ, I pray. Amen.

That's my 2 cents.

Love,
Mom

Father's Day

June 15, 2014

Dear Liberty,

I was looking at a Father's Day pictorial tribute on the Internet when I noticed the word "partner" was used instead of wife. It reminded me that God does want a man and woman to be partners, but it is so much more than that.

"Then the LORD God said, 'It is not good that the man should be alone; I will make him a helper fit for him.'" Genesis 2:18

The original Hebrew text for "helper", or ezer k'enegdo, is translated more accurately as "help meet". Looking even deeper, the root of ezer is "to be strong" or "strength". K'enegdo is only used in this passage in the Bible and means "in front of", "opposite" or "exactly corresponding to".

Those wanting to discredit the Bible misuse passages like this to imply the Bible describes women as inferior to men. In truly studying and understanding God's Word and desire for his children you realize that our Heavenly Father was actually creating someone who was not only equal to but also completed Adam. Someone who was opposite but exactly corresponded to him, like a mirror image. God designed Eve to be Adam's reflective opposite, not a carbon copy of Adam, possessing the qualities, characteristics, functions and attributes that he did not have. Adam and Eve were equivalent but different. Men and women were meant to complement each other and when the two come together, they become one.

"Therefore a man shall leave his father and his mother and hold fast to his wife, and they shall become one flesh." Genesis 2:24

Now, God also said, "Be fruitful and multiply." You will hear this story time and time again over the years but everyone who knew your father before you were born knew he did not want children. There was no interest there at all, mainly because he understood the awesome responsibility parents have in raising their children. But Liberty, from the moment your father found out God had blessed us with you, he could not have been prouder. He displayed your first ultrasound photo at work, he took amazing care of me and treated me like a queen, and he bragged to anybody who would listen about the amazing little girl he was going to have. For a man who never wanted children I never saw more love, more affection, and more pride from anyone than what I saw in your father from the moment he first laid eyes on you.

You are too little right now to understand Father's Day, but I hope over the years you come to appreciate to opportunity to recognize how wonderful your daddy is. Liberty, your earthly father is a sinful man. He makes mistakes and he can be difficult sometimes, but he is one of the most Godly men you will ever know. He's my strength when I am vulnerable, he gives me courage when I feel like a coward, he's my light when I'm in darkness, and he is always the Stiller to my Meara. He is tender, cool-headed, and forgiving, but he will correct you when he believes you are in error. He will also teach you the most important thing you will ever know, the love and compassion of your Heavenly Father and how He sent His only begotten son to die for your sins so that you may live with Him for eternity.

There is a saying that woman are attracted to men who remind them of their fathers. Liberty, if that is true, you will be blessed. But come what may remember that the relationship with your Heavenly Father is the most important relationship of all and He will be there for you no matter what. And for those times you need someone here on earth to hold you and tell you it's all right, or to sneak you a piece of gum when mommy's not looking, He gave you a daddy who loves you more than any daddy could every love his little girl.

That's my 2 cents.

Love,
Mom

Sleeping Beauty

June 21, 2014

Dear Liberty,

I watched you sleep today. You are so beautiful. I saw your little eyes flitter in dream. I listened to your breathing while your chest raised and lowered. I noticed your little fingers twitch and was overcome with love for you.

As I watched, I considered the multitude of muscles, tissues and intricate pieces that make up your little body. I pondered all the amazing things that have to come together to make you work. The miles of veins that take blood from your heart to every other part of you and back again. I thought of your little brain and how much you have already learned in your two short years and how much more you have to go. I contemplated the 200 separate components in your eyes working in concert to make those beautiful baby blues shine.

Glancing over to one of your recent favorite books, <u>The Tooth Book</u> by Dr. Seuss, I was humbled by the fact that we are given two sets of teeth like most mammals. How fascinating it is that the body knows to grow a set and after a standard amount of time those teeth fall out on their own and a new set grows in.

My thoughts wondered to your little stomach and how much it can actually hold. You are your father's daughter, you know. There are acids in your stomach so powerful that if a drop were placed on a piece of wood it would eat right through it, yet it does not disturb your tissue. It amazes me how incredible the human body is.

Inevitably I began to meditate how you became you. We are told that science proves humans evolved to our current form over millions of years. Ok. Can science prove how the central nervous system developed? How did the sensory lines form and work their way all through the body to send messages to the brain? How did the body know that it needed two sets of teeth and how did that second set develop? Has science demonstrated how the fish developed lungs and was able to begin breathing through the nose instead of gills? Can science replicate the process that allowed the reptile, an egg-laying creature, to turn into a mammal, a live-birthing creature, or are we forced to just accept millions of years of evolution without any definitive proof? (see <u>When Does Life Begin?</u>-Vol.2)

Many will tell you the monotreme is evidence of that transition as they are egg-laying mammals. Ok, but where is the transformation from reptile to monotreme and more importantly, how did the monotreme evolve into a creature that birthed their offspring? If it took millions of years, where are the fossils of all the missing links between the specimens we do have? If it was spontaneous evolution, why do we not have examples of that happening now? Also, not only would a male have to undergo the necessary changes to evolve, a female would have to identically mimic those changes as well so the new species could be reproduced. What are the odds?

Liberty, you are going to be faced with people demanding there is a consensus regarding evolution. The claim itself is a huge red flag that something is wrong with this theory as discussed in my letter entitled <u>Is Consensus Always Right</u>? As science is always changing and new evidence is continuously being discovered, they will never have consensus in science, nor should there be. This reality will lead some to call you a hater of science. On the contrary, it is because of science, because of the extraordinary discovers made about our anatomy every day, that the thought of millions of complex components accidentally coming together at just the right moment to form the human body proves to be more and more impossible as we go along. By their own admission, many evolutionists know this to be true but accepting the alternative is not a possibility for them. They would rather devote themselves to a lie than accept God.

Dr. George Wald, a Professor of Biology at the University of Harvard, Nobel Prize winner in medicine and stanch evolutionist, said it best. "There are only two possibilities as to how life arose; one is spontaneous generation arising to evolution, the other is a supernatural creative act of God, there is no third possibility. Spontaneous generation in which life arose from non-living matter was scientifically disproved 120 years ago by Louis Pasteur and others. That leaves us with only one possible conclusion that life arose as a creative act of God. I will not accept that philosophically because I do not want to believe in God, therefore I choose to believe in that which I know is scientifically impossible, spontaneous generation arising to evolution." "One has only to contemplate the magnitude of this task to concede that the spontaneous generation of a living organism is impossible. Yet we are here—as a result, I believe, of spontaneous generation."

Militant anti-Christian physical anthropologist Sir Arthur Keith declared, "Evolution is unproved and improvable, we believe it because the only alternative is special creation, which is unthinkable."

Many will say that there is no credible evidence that creation is possible. There's plenty of evidence supporting creationism but those entering the discussion with their results already concluded are the ones dismissing any oppositional proof. If you refuse to accept a creator then any evidence supporting that will be outrageous to you. Even Charles Darwin acknowledged reservations in his own theory in his book *The Origin of Species by Means of Natural Selection*. "To suppose that the eye, with all its inimitable contrivances for adjusting the focus to different distances, for admitting different amounts of light, and for the correction of spherical and chromatic aberration, could have formed by natural selection, seems, I freely confess, absurd in the highest degree possible." Yet even today his theory is indoctrinated as fact.

Understand, Liberty, there is a very dangerous practice happening with modern "science". The study of science requires one develop a scientific hypothesis, test that hypothesis and then draw conclusions depending on the results i.e. is the hypothesis correct? Finding support for a hypothesis is not really science. Proving a hypothesis true is achieved by conducting experiments to DISPROVE the theory. Unfortunately, too many people with an agenda are trying to use "science" to satisfy the conclusions they want and call any results contrary to that thesis false science, agenda driving, religious based and outright stupid. Only experiments and discoveries yielding the outcomes supporting their theory are quoted, while discarding any facts disproving their thesis. This is not science.

The truth is there are hundreds of studies being published questioning the evolutionary theory, but teachers are being reprimanded for daring to even discuss them in schools. Why? That is what science is all about. Showing both sides, examining all evidence and determining the best conclusion. That is not achieved when one is only given a specific, skewed amount of information and told it is definitive. When this happens, someone is hiding something.

Use your brain, my dear Liberty, that so called 'evolutionary' wonder. Think for yourself. Never accept what someone tells you as truth without researching it yourself, especially information that disproves the theory. Never be afraid to challenge someone on their beliefs, but make sure to do it with respect and love. Better yet, know all the positions of a philosophy so you can argue their beliefs better than they can, but then show them where that opinion may be incorrect. For example, the best way to discuss evolution with someone is to know the arguments for evolution and what the theory really teaches. You'd be surprised how many people say they believe humans evolved from apes but really have no idea what evolution is truly advocating, starting with primordial soup.

Scientifically we can show that no species has ever transformed into another species, yet this is the basis of evolution. Science also *confirms that genetic mutations never add information to DNA but always subtracts, contrary to a fundamental evolutionary requirement.*

Hold to truth, Liberty. Always hold to truth and facts. In this case is it scientific proof of evolution or is it an outright denial of God? Remember Satan is always trying to persuade you with his original question, "Did God really say that?" Yes, Liberty, yes He did.

That's my 2 cents.

Love,
Mom

The Candy Bomber

June 24, 2014

Dear Liberty,

I hear many argue these days there is no such thing as American compassion. Those serving in Germany 66 years ago today would have evidence otherwise.

The end of the European conflict of World War II on May 8, 1945, or V-E Day as Americans call it, sparked the beginning of the Cold War. After the surrender of Germany, the Western Allies made an agreement with the Soviet Union to allocate control of Germany among the forces fighting the Nazis. The western portion of Germany was to be occupied by the democratic Allies while the east was occupied by the Soviet Union. This also applied to the capital of Berlin. Unfortunately Berlin was located 100 miles inside the Soviet Union controlled section of Germany.

In 1939, Joseph Stalin of the Soviet Union and Adolph Hitler of Germany were actually working together invading neighboring countries. Stalin, a leader in the communist movement, and Hitler, a champion of the socialist movement, saw common ground in their beliefs of world domination. Stalin was more than agreeable when Hitler approached him for support in invading Poland. He even returned Jews fleeing to Russia for Hitler to confine in concentration camps. Having starved millions of Ukrainians himself, tossing them in mass graves, Stalin had no issue with Hitler or his treatment of Jews. That is, until June of 1941 when Hitler dared to invade parts of the Soviet Union. After 2 years of fighting his one time comrade, Stalin meet with President Franklin D. Roosevelt and British Prime Minister Winston Churchill (see The British Bulldog-Vol.3) in November of 1943 at the Tehran Conference to discuss a coalition. They began a 2-front offensive against Germany. Because of this alliance, the United States, Britain, France and the Soviet Union received controlling portions of Germany after it's surrender. Originally France was denied any part of Germany but the United States and Britain wished to recognize Frances' contributions to the war and each gave a portion of their territories to their ally.

While capitalist America was trying to help Germany become stable and prosperous again, the communist Soviet Union had other plans. Three years after V-E Day Stalin began flexing his muscles and orchestrated the Berlin Blockade. In efforts to choke Germany's economic growth, on June 24, 1948, the Soviet Union began blocking all Western Allies' land transport routes, including roads, railways, and canals, to their respective portions of Berlin risking the lives of 2 million people. Their goal was to force the Western Allies to purchase supplies for Berlin from the Soviet Union which would all but guarantee total control of the city to the superpower. They wanted to ensure not only their occupied territory but also all of Berlin to become a communist stronghold. Convinced America would soon withdraw from Germany all together, Stalin was working with German communist leaders to force hardship and struggle on all Germans so as to unite the country completely under communist and Soviet control.

The Western Allied forces, understanding the humanitarian crisis evolving, quickly organized the Berlin Airlift and began flying supplies to the citizens of West Berlin a few days later. Air Forces from the United States, Britain, Canada, Australia, New Zealand and South Africa flew 270,000 flights during the 1-year blockade, supplying up to 4700 tons of fuel and food daily to Berlin. This is not the end of the charitable story of the people of America though.

The children of Berlin would often gather at the end of runways to watch supply planes land and take off. One day an American pilot approached these children to talk. Knowing they were hungry he reached into his pocket only to find just 2 sticks of gum. Disappointed he didn't have more, he gave the children what he had. Without hesitation or argument the children began sharing the gum and enjoy what little piece they were given. Overcome with compassion, Gail S. "Hal" Halvorsen promised to bring more candy on his next flight and drop it to them from the sky. Since planes were arriving every 3 minutes the children asked how they would know which plane was his. He responded, "I will wiggle my wings."

"Uncle Wiggle Wings" Halvorsen returned to base to gather as much candy as he could. As promised he started dropping the candy attached to handkerchief parachutes during his next flight. His fellow pilots and crewmen donated candy and dubbed him the "Candy Bomber." As attention grew, Halvorsen's commanding officer, Lt. General William H. Turner, ordered "Operation Little Vittles" sparking widespread media attention. Public support exploded in the states prompting donations from individuals like school children to companies such as the Confectioners Association of America. By the end of the blockade, Uncle Wiggle Wings, with the help of approximately 25 other crews, had dropped 23 tons of chewing gum, chocolates and other candy to the children of Berlin.

By April 1949, the Berlin Airlift campaign was so successful it was supplying more cargo than the railroad had been before the blockade. The Soviet Union was forced to lift the ban a month later to *avoid further humiliation from the capitalist allies. As a result of this incident, Germany was split into two separate German states instead of just occupied territories. West Germany became the Federal Republic of Germany and East Germany was designated the German Democratic Republic, which is quite ironic as it was under communist control. This was the first of many peaceful conflicts between the Soviet Union and the United States.*

Liberty, you will always find forces in this world, whether international or domestic, that have interests in exerting dominance over the people. There will always be someone out there trying to grab as much control as he or she can. You have a weapon, Liberty, that can defeat this force at every turn. It is called love. Love for God and love for your fellow man whether they live next door or 4,000 miles away. While dictators desperately force people into groups, remember to concentrate on the individual. Show love, show courage, show compassion and you will foster hope, foster kindness, and change the world.

That's my 2 cents.

Love,
Mom

The Birth of a Movement

June 29, 2014

Dear Liberty,

Political division has split the country in two. Citizens are losing faith in both parties. Politicians make promises declaring their ideologies but power and personal gain overwhelm any pledge uttered during a campaign upon arrival to Washington. A principled group emerged demanding their cries be heard yet they were beaten down, literally, by commanding politicians including those in their own party. No, I'm not talking about today and I'm not talking about the Tea Party.

Raised by a lawyer and abolitionist, Charles Sumner was brought up understanding the inhumanities of slavery and the necessity for equality of all regardless of race. Believing contentious views between blacks and whites were indoctrinated, not instinctive, he became an outspoken anti-slavery activist. He challenged the legality of segregated schools in Massachusetts by representing black parents, lead by Benjamin Roberts, in Roberts vs. Boston. Searching for a political party that shared his anti-slavery views, Charles lead the Conscience Whigs of Massachusetts for a short time until the Whig party nominated slave-owner Zachary Taylor for President. He organized the Free Soil Party in response, which opposed both Democrats and Whigs.

Forming an alliance with his state legislature Democrats despite objections by some to his radical views, they elected Charles U.S. Senator in 1851 as a Free Soil Democrat by one vote. Remaining uncontroversial at first, Charles began powerfully voicing his anti-slavery views in his second year, an opinion which most in the U.S. Senate did not appreciate regardless of political affiliation.

As the young country expanded and territories were created, pro- and anti-slavery advocates were fighting hard to seize these new regions ensuring more national political power. To avoid having to take a stand, Democrat Senators Stephen A. Douglas of Illinois and Andrew Butler of South Carolina devised the Kansas-Nebraska Act of 1854 allowing settlers to decide the future of their area despite the fact that Kansas was already designated a free state. This resulted in a massive flood of Southern pro-slavery and Northern anti-slavery proponents to Kansas competing for votes to decide the fate of the territory in their favor. The ramifications were violent battles between settlers. In trying to keep their hands clean, politicians ultimately caused an extremely bloody war dubbed the "Bleeding Kansas" crisis. Fed up with legislators vowing to end slavery without following through, the Kansas-Nebraska Act motivated a handful of honest anti-slavery politicians from all parties to band together. They called themselves Republicans.

It was in response to the Kansas bloodshed that Charles Sumner, a leader in the new party, took to the Senate floor in May of 1856 to deliver his "Crime against Kansas" speech. He spoke passionately against "Slave Power", the anti-slavery charge of disproportionate legislative control in the national government by wealthy slave owners who used that political power to force slavery in free states. Taking the fight to the authors of the Act, Charles had strong words against both Stephen Douglas and Andrew Butler. Referring to Senator Douglas, Charles said, "Not in any common lust for power did this uncommon tragedy have its origin. It is the rape of a virgin Territory, compelling it to the hateful embrace of slavery; and it may be clearly traced to a depraved desire for a new Slave State, hideous offspring of such a crime, in the hope of adding to the power of slavery in the National Government."

If that were not enough, Charles turned his attention to Senator Butler saying, "The senator from South Carolina has read many books of chivalry, and believes himself a chivalrous knight with sentiments of honor and courage. Of course he has chosen a mistress to whom he has made his vows, and who, though ugly to others, is always lovely to him; though polluted in the sight of the world, is chaste in his sight -- I mean the harlot, slavery. For her his tongue is always profuse in words. Let her be impeached in character, or any proposition made to shut her out from the extension of her wantonness, and no extravagance of manner or hardihood of assertion is then too great for this senator."

A relative of Andrew Butler, South Carolina Representative Preston Brooks took exception to the comments about his kinsman and state and approached Senator Sumner in the Senate Chambers two days following the speech. After expressing his displeasure verbally, Preston raised his cane and began beating Charles on the head with all the force he could gather. Despite Charles falling to the ground, blinded by his own blood, Preston did not halt the thrashing until his cane finally broke. Then with confidence and assurance, Rep. Brooks turned and freely walked out of the chambers while people scrambled to help the unconscious Sumner. Preston eventually resigned but he was a hero to his constituents. The South rallied behind their statesman, sending him canes and re-electing him to his position. Northern abolitionists and equal civil rights activists saw the integrity in Charles Sumner and began entrusting their political support in those who were serious about ending slavery and giving blacks equal rights, the new Republican Party. Within a few years the young party had obtained the White House with the election of Abraham Lincoln, the first Republican president.

Liberty, we are at a time again where both political parties are so drunk with power they are ignoring the voice of the people. This was undoubtedly exhibited in the recent Mississippi Republican primary run-off. The Republican establishment candidate, Thad Cochran, actually turned to questionable, possibly illegal tactics to defeat Republican Tea Party candidate Chris McDaniel. While it is perfectly acceptable to reach across the aisle during a general election, it is quite underhanded to lie and deceive opposing party members, who have no intention on voting for you in the general election, to come and vote for you in your own primary. We are once again fighting the "Slave Power" in Washington. The federal slave owners are putting their foot on the necks of all Americans in efforts to overpower any freedom that may still exist and enslave us all on the big government plantation.

Can we not see political similarities today in the words written almost 160 years ago? The Cincinnati Gazette opined, "The South cannot tolerate free speech anywhere, and would stifle it in Washington with the bludgeon and the bowie-knife, as they are now trying to stifle it in Kansas by massacre, rapine, and murder." New York Evening Post's William Cullen Bryant asked, "Has it come to this, that we must speak with bated breath in the presence of our Southern masters?... Are we to be chastised as they chastise their slaves? Are we too, slaves, slaves for life, a target for their brutal blows, when we do not comport ourselves to please them?" Today we are being choked by the tenets of political correctness with the press happily slaughtering any dissenters with their pen.

In the South, Preston supporters gleefully expressed their approval of the caning suggesting this should be common practice to all who oppose them. The Richmond Enquirer condemned "these vulgar abolitionists in the Senate" who "have been suffered to run too long without collars. They must be lashed into submission." If you replaced "abolitionists" with "Tea Partiers", this sentiment could be posted in any liberal newspaper of your choice receiving cheers and adoration as many today echo this attitude about anyone who dares question their progressive, suppressing policies.

Shortly after Preston's re-election he died at the age of 37. Massachusetts General Council re-elected Sumner in 1856 even though he was still recovering from the incident. It was believed that the empty seat was a powerful statement of freedom of speech. Sumner returned to the Senate in 1859 after a 5-year absence in time to support Abraham Lincoln's presidential campaign. Standing on principle, when advised by fellow Republicans to take a less forceful tone, Charles answered, "When crime and criminals are thrust before us, they are to be met by all the energies that God has given us by argument, scorn, sarcasm and denunciation." Liberty, Charles has a point here. We are to fight the forces of evil with the energies of God, but maybe not with all the tactics Charles suggests. We are to continue to speak the truth with confidence and faith as demonstrated by Sen. Sumner on June 4, 1860, in his first speech since his return entitled, <u>The Barbarism of Slavery</u>. He boldly forged ahead with his crusade to denounce slavery, forcefully arguing it's inhumanity. He remained in the Senate through the Civil War, working diligently to end slavery, often speaking to President Lincoln about emancipating the slaves. He represented his state until his death in 1874, 15 years after his return from the caning.

Liberty, standing up for what is right is not easy. You will face opposition every step of the way. You will be mocked, ridiculed, and attacked verbally and possibly physically. Truth is truth, though, and right is right. When you have moments of weakness, look to the cross. Remember the suffering our Lord and Savior Jesus Christ endured for us, while we were still sinners, to sanctify us and give us the gift of eternal life.

> Be still before the Lord and wait patiently for him;
> do not fret when people succeed in their ways,
> when they carry out their wicked schemes.
> Refrain from anger and turn from wrath;
> do not fret—it leads only to evil.
> For those who are evil will be destroyed,
> but those who hope in the Lord will inherit the land.
> (Psalms 37:7-9)

That's my 2 cents.

Love,
Mom

Happy Independence Day

July 4, 2014

Dear Liberty,

"The second day of July 1776 will be the most memorable epoch in the history of America. I am apt to believe that it will be celebrated by succeeding generations as the great anniversary festival. It ought to be commemorated as the day of deliverance, by solemn acts of devotion to God Almighty. It ought to be solemnized with pomp and parade, with shows, games, sports, guns, bells, bonfires, and illuminations, from one end of this continent to the other, from this time forward forever.

"You will think me transported with enthusiasm, but I am not. I am well aware of the toil and blood and treasure that it will cost to maintain this Declaration and support and defend these States. Yet through all the gloom I can see the rays of ravishing light and glory. I can see that the end is worth more than all the means; that posterity will triumph in that day's transaction, even though we [may regret] it, which I trust in God we shall not."

John Adams wrote this sentiment to his wife in a letter dated July 3, 1776, after the first draft of the Declaration of Independence was presented to Congress. Characterizing the historical significance of the event perfectly, he missed the date by two days due to the fact that the final version of the Declaration was not officially adopted until July 4, 1776. Interestingly enough, not all signed the document on the 4th with some disputing any signed that day at all, though Jefferson, Adams and Franklin all declared they did endorse the Declaration on July 4th.

But what is it that makes this document so amazing, so historical, and so unprecedented that even today tyrants fear it and liberty-loving people all over the world risk everything to come to America and live under it? America has a vibrant, rich history including both good and bad moments, but we are unique in the principle of giving the power to the governed, not the government.

Some of the most remarkable proclamations are made in the 2nd paragraph of this declaration:

"We hold these truths to be self-evident" - They are obvious, unmistakable, and undeniable. Undeniable, Liberty. That means no one can take them away from you.

"That all men are created equal" - No matter race, creed or color, every person is CREATED equal. That does not mean everyone achieves equal pay or an equal house or equal wealth. It means we are all born as God's children and considering one inferior because of race or religion or nationality is against God's plan for all humans. Abolitionists proclaimed this as a pronouncement by our Founding Fathers that slaves were white man's equals. Unfortunately the phrase does not guarantee that humans will be void of conflict and war because this world habitually chooses to not follow God's plan.

"That they are endowed by their Creator" - Yes, Liberty, our Founding Fathers DID believe in God, in a Creator. Many today are working tirelessly to re-write history, removing references to God from our Founding Fathers' mouths and pens. They focus on Thomas Jefferson, who many argue was not a Christian but a deist. <u>The Life and Morals of Jesus of Nazareth</u>, or the Jefferson Bible as it is informally called, was a collection of passages from the gospels that Jefferson selected and pasted together himself. Since he left out miracles and the Resurrection, many claim he was a denier of the true Christ. The truth is his book focused on the teachings of Christ and Jefferson believed it was a model for Christian morality. If the people conducted their lives with these virtues then they have the tools to govern themselves and not be enslaved by a government.

In addition to the Jefferson misrepresentation, it is also conveniently ignored that 23 out of 56 signers were clergy so I would argue that prayers, Judeo-Christian principles and Christ's name were enthusiastically welcomed in the government, not aggressively denied. This country was founded by people who wanted Freedom OF Religion, not Freedom FROM Religion. It was undoubtedly founded by people who spoke of Christ and God both in government and in their lives, not just in their churches. That is why Moses holding the 10 Commandments is etched into the Supreme Court building. Our forefathers proclaimed in the Declaration that there are certain freedoms given by God and because of that, no one can deny them. It is this concept that made the Declaration of Independence so historical and so unique. Until then people were resigned to accept their rights were granted to them by a government or king, which allowed that government or king to take them away. There are many today who must remove God from our lives and our history so they can once again assume the role of ultimate authority.

"with certain unalienable Rights" - Freedoms that cannot ever be taken away from you and rights that you can't even give away.

"that among these are Life" - Life, that precious gift that God gives us from conception. That priceless unalienable right that pro-abortion supporerts take from hundreds of thousands of humans every year. Life, that treasured gift from God that we have a right to protect with any means necessary, including a gun, if it is threatened.

"Liberty" - Independence, freedom, and self-determination to decide your own direction, your own path, and your own destiny. Socialism, while claiming to work for the greater good, grabs freedom at every turn. You can't homeschool because it's not fair. You can't have that car because it uses too much gas. You can't carry a gun to protect yourself because someone might get hurt. You must pay for abortions because women deserve health care. You must not only accept, but your church must also perform same-sex marriage otherwise you are a hater. You must believe in global warming and pay extraordinary taxes to combat it. Liberty, these are the issues your parents are fighting today in efforts to save liberty in America for you and your children. It's what all these letters are about. God be with us in this struggle.

"and the pursuit of Happiness" - Most people do not know but the original phrase used here was "pursuit of Property". Since owning property is a form of happiness to many, the pursuit of it is considered a right. Our Founding Fathers, in their wisdom and attempts by many to advance a path of eradicating slavery, saw a danger in this wording and replaced the term "property" so slave-owners could not claim that owning a slave, which they considered property, was a Constitutional right. What does "Pursuit of Happiness" mean, though? Does it guarantee you will be happy? Does it swear you will make a lot of money? Does it promise you will be successful? Does it ensure you will have a lot of processions? No, no, no and no. It means you have the right to actively strive for whatever makes you satisfied. You have the privilege to forge ahead with any past-time, faith, career, or invention you desire but take heed not to get deceived into believing you are assured success.

"That to secure these rights, Governments are instituted among Men, deriving their just powers from the consent of the governed." - Never before had the power of the government been put into the hands of those who are governed. Under this provision Americans have the responsibility to hold our elected officials accountable for their actions. We are to watch them diligently and speak out when we see the government doing anything to overrule the rights given to us by God, stated in the Constitution and entrusted to the government to protect. That, Liberty, is why today's Constitutionalists are so feared by both the Left and the Right in Washington. Constitutionalists are the defenders of the Constitution and the educators of the ignorant. They are America.

In 1780, John Adams wrote to his wife, Abigail, "I must study politics and war that my sons may have liberty to study mathematics and philosophy. My sons ought to study mathematics and philosophy, geography, natural history and naval architecture, navigation, commerce and agriculture, in order to give their children a right to study painting, poetry, music, architecture, statuary, tapestry, and porcelain."

One can argue we have gone full circle and have spent so much time studying painting, poetry, music, etc that we have forgotten the beauty and significance of studying mathematics and philosophy and we have neglected the necessity and understanding of studying politics and war. I believe we are at a time again where America is rebooting itself, clearing out all the viruses and bugs in the government and returning to the original operating system.

Liberty, your father and I are studying politics and war that you may have liberty to study mathematics and philosophy in order to give your children a right to study painting, poetry, music, architecture, statuary, tapestry, and porcelain. May God be with us today as he was with us over 200 years ago.

That's my 2 cents.

Love,
Mom

July 13, 2014

Dear Liberty,

Over the past month the United States has experienced an enormous influx of illegal aliens from Central and South America, with an overwhelming number of unaccompanied minors in the mix of extremely violent gang members and terrorists. While the administration says it is working on a situation, boarder towns are being flooded, the feds are transporting hundreds of illegals all over America dumping them in cities with just a few hours notice, boarder agents are threatened with their jobs if they talk about or take pictures of what is happening, only Democrat Congressmen pushing amnesty are allowed to visit the refugee camps, threatening diseases are being re-introduced to the country in record numbers, and boarder guards are commanded to stand down and allow easy access to those crossing the boarder. In the meantime, the President is traveling the country fundraising and demanding amnesty. He even had three events in Texas but refused to visit any boarder town.

Conservative radio and TV personality Glenn Beck has ruffled a few feathers of his own as he has decided to take help to the churches and towns crying for relieve from this onslaught. Mind you he is also still calling for the return of these lawbreakers to their countries. What is quite interesting is how many of his frequent listeners are very much in disagreement with his decision to go to the boarder with food and toys while those who never have a kind word about him are agreeing with his action and calling him Christ-like. This sparks a very interesting debate.

As Christians we are suppose to love our enemies as well as our neighbors and help them in their time of need. But at what point does helping someone actually encourage their bad, and in this case illegal and dangerous, behavior? I would like to put the Christian argument on the back burner for just a moment and look at this situation from a different angle.

As a conservative my principles have always stemmed from the belief that government should be as uninvolved as possible with as minimal power imaginable. To have that tenet one must accept responsibility falls on individual citizens, churches and charities to look after the poor, the hungry, and yes, sometimes even the lawbreakers. When an administration wants to acquire power from the people, a crisis is often created and upon people demanding a solution, those in power raise their fists and smash individual freedom to bits.

The citizens of America must stand up, roll up their sleeves and work together to overcome this inundation of not only children but vicious gang members and radical extremists. If we do, how much stronger will our voices be when we stand hand in hand with the children we have fed and clothed and then say, "We love them, but they must be sent back home." Those who continue to just fight against the government with words will be demeaned by politicians as doing nothing to solve the problem. And the politicians will be right. We must fight with our actions as well as our words.

Returning to the matter of What Would Jesus Do?, there are several examples of Christ's behavior being referenced as evidence for one point of view or the other. Those supporting efforts to help the boarder towns recite the Good Samaritan story as well as all the dinners and gatherings Jesus had with prostitutes, tax collectors, and basically the worst sinners he could find. Others recall moments of Jesus' anger as confirmation that we cannot support this behavior in any way.

While Jesus did turn tables over in the temple and rebuked church leaders, one must remember the context of those cases. Jesus was reprimanding those who knew the law, even taught the law, not to mention the leaders of the people. They were the ones intended by God to be ministering to the prostitutes, tax collectors and sinners themselves, but they were too saturated with power and the desire for more to listen to the truth. Hence, Jesus' anger in their stubbornness and lawlessness.

So which examples of Jesus do we follow? Both. When Jesus saved the adulterer, he did not overlook her actions. He told her, "Go and sin no more." We do not overlook the actions of the children or adults entering this country illegally. We can love them but let them know they must not sin, or break the law, anymore. Whose hearts did Jesus touch more deeply, the leaders or the sinners? But more importantly, who were more likely to turn from their sins after Jesus' demonstration of love?

America is great because Americans are great. We need to be greater now than we've ever been before. Americans have always extended a hand to all nations, convinced it is our moral obligation to help those everywhere in the world when we can. This is a principled understanding possessed by believers and non-believers alike by the mere fact our country was founded on Judeo-Christian *standards. These ethics are woven into the fabric of our culture that all have benefited from regardless of race, creed, color or nationality.*

We the People can take power back from the government, including Congress, by doing the right thing ourselves. That is why churches are opening their doors to feed and clothe the children. Meanwhile, militias from all over the country are going to the boarder to stand hand in hand in efforts to stop the hemorrhaging of those entering America illegally. If the government won't do this one, Constitutionally commanded duty, then Americans will. So when the politicians try to say we need legislation to correct the problem, we will have every evidence to say, "Why? We already solved it."

That, my dear Liberty, is how you keep your freedom.

That's my 2 cents.

Love,
Mom

Man On the Moon

July 20, 2014

Dear Liberty,

"That's one small step for a man; one giant leap for mankind."

Exactly one year before your father and I were born, Commander Neil Armstrong spoke this unforgettable phrase. Our generation knows these words intimately along with the significance of man's first steps on the moon. But the day before Armstrong put his foot on the moon and spoke these words to the world, Colonel Edwin "Buzz" Aldrin, the Lunar Module Pilot, made an even more noteworthy statement in the privacy of their spacecraft.

On the morning of the Lunar landing 45 years ago today, Buzz transmitted the following message to NASA headquarters in Houston, Texas. "This is the LM pilot speaking. I would like to request a few moments of silence. I'd like to take this opportunity to ask every person listening in, whoever or wherever they may be, to pause for a moment and contemplate the events of the past few hours, and to give thanks in his own individual way." After which the radio went silent. During this time, Buzz took a tiny travel communion set his church gave him, celebrated the Holy Sacrament and recited John 15:5 which reads, "I am the vine, you are the branches. He who abides in Me, and I in him, bears much fruit." Buzz later commented that, "It was interesting to think that the very first liquid ever poured on the moon, and the first food eaten there, were communion elements." More specifically, the body and blood of our Lord and Savior Jesus Christ.

It is so humbling to imagine that America and mankind traveled from their very first flight on December 17, 1903 to the moon just 66 years later on July 20, 1969. Technology is such an amazing gift from God, blessing humanity and our country. America is not an accident. America is not just another country. America is a dream and it is hope for a better tomorrow.

Many progressives today are trying to shame white Americans into believing they are thieving, deceitful, greedy people. One of their most despised phrases is "American Exceptionalism." They accuse Americans of claiming to be better than other countries. But Liberty, that is not what American Exceptionalism means at all. It's the aspiration to find a way to soar with the eagles and not stop till we shine with the stars. It's the passion to say, "Let me show you what I can do, just give me the freedom to do it." It's knowing our parents and our grandparents had a hard life, allowing us the liberty to choose our own occupation, determine our own path, so that we could work even harder and make a better life for ourselves and our children.

We are not better than citizens of other countries, but we were founded on a principle unique from every other county. "Give me your tired, your poor, and your huddled masses yearning to breathe free." We do not cry for the lords and nobility, for the wealthy and affluent, or the privileged few, no more than we solicit those who what to live off the backs of others. Instead we summon individuals who hunger to be released from the shackles of their respective monarchies and dictators and long to govern themselves. Give us those who yearn "to breathe free," not yearn to get life for free. That is why America is exceptional. It is our eagerness and enthusiasm to make the world better and our inalienable, self-evident right to be free. It's what we think, what we believe, what we know we can do for ourselves and others if we are just given the chance.

"And so, my fellow Americans: ask not what your country can do for you - ask what you can do for your country. My fellow citizens of the world: ask not what America will do for you, but what together we can do for the freedom of man."

This was President Kennedy's philosophy which led him to propose to Congress the goal of America "landing a man on the moon and returning him safely to the earth" within 8 years. A goal which was pursued and achieved by hardworking, innovative and extraordinary individuals. America's desire has never been to conquer and dominate the world but to bring the world along with her on her journey. This is what sets her apart and makes her exceptional.

But above all that, Liberty, has been the United State's acknowledgement of our blessings from our Father in Heaven since our inception. The humility of knowing our only King, our only ruler, is our Creator. As Buzz recognized, it is under the loving, supporting hand of our God that we are blessed with such prosperity, such achievements, and such good fortunes.

We are at a very fragile time when many wish to erase God from *not only our present and our future, but they are actively expunging Him from our past. If we continue down this path and refuse to turn back to God, our tower of Babel will crumble so fast and so far that we will long for the days of the 19th century because of their outstanding luxuries.*

Thank you Neil Armstrong, Buzz Aldrin, and Michael Collins for being such fearless pioneers and an amazing example of the heart and soul of America. A special thank you to Buzz for taking pause during this incredible moment in history to recognize and give thanks to the one who made it possible. May we return to those days of seeking to improve America instead of apologizing for her. If we do, we will truly be blessed and can thank God every step of the way.

That's my 2 cents.

Love,
Mom

America's Pale Blue Trabant

July 24, 2014

Dear Liberty,

 When people think about the finest cars in the world, German automobiles act as the gold standard. No matter the manufacturer, if they want to claim performance and luxury they have to compete with the very best that the Germans have to offer. BMW lets buyers know what they're getting through their slogans, "The Ultimate Driving Machine" and "Sheer Driving Pleasure." Porsche's motto is very clear, "Porsche, there is no substitute." Mercedes-Benz tags itself as "The Future of the Automobile." Finally, Audi makes the bold claim that, "Everyone dreams of an Audi."

 Perhaps it's not surprising that Germany produces some of the finest cars in the world. Karl Benz invented the automobile, so they did have a head start on the rest of the world. The four-stroke engine and the diesel engine were both created in Germany and remain the basic design in most cars even today. Ferdinand Porsche designed the original Volkswagen which brought the 'people's car' to the masses.

 Even at your age, when we go anywhere you say, "Beemer!" with the delight of a 2-year-old car aficionado. Owning a couple of BMWs you know that a ten-year-old 'Beemer' is as desirable as a brand new car from about any other manufacturer out there. World-class design and engineering combined with top of the line materials leads to a product that stands the test of time. With the high speeds driven on the Autobahn, power and handling combined with the ultimate in comfort are simply an expectation, not a goal.

 But at one time, Germany was also known for producing the worst car ever created. The basic car remained unchanged for nearly 30 years with 3,000,000 cars rolling, or more accurately, being pushed off the assembly line. It had enough room for four adults and a 600 cc 2-cycle engine producing a staggering 26 horsepower, allowing it to blast to 60 mph in 21 seconds and achieve a top speed of 70 mph. Despite the engine's diminutive size, it produced nine times the amount of pollution as an average car, even though the competing engine was ten times more powerful. To fill the gas tank required popping the hood, filling the tank with gas and 2-cycle oil, and then rocking the car to combine the mixture. Much of the car's body was produced from recycled materials and the waiting list for a new automobile was often

15 years, making used models frequently more expensive than new one's as they were readily available for sale.

The car was called the Trabant. Although it was produced for 3 decades and with millions of copies built, it may very well have been the single worst car ever to wheeze off an assembly line. What separated the Trabant from the high quality automobiles that Germany is known for? It's very simple. It was the wall that ran through the middle of Germany. The wall that separated the East from the West, the free from the oppressed.

In West Germany auto manufactures competed on racetracks to outperform the competition, living by the motto, "Race on Sunday, sell on Monday." Quality developed simply because the better the performance and design of their cars, the more cars they would sell.

In East Germany, the situation was quite different. In the East, there was no need to compete, the options that consumers could choose from totaled one, and you could have it in any color that you wanted, as long as it was pale blue. Without the need to compete, the Trabant had little need to improve through its thirty years of production. The fact that it remained little changed over its lifetime certainly didn't mean that it started out as the perfect car. In fact, when the "Berlin Wall" fell, the little Trabant carried many of their owners slowly west through the concrete wall that divided the country and were promptly abandoned when the owner finally tasted freedom.

Yet, where does the US find itself heading today? In many ways we're taking our Hummers and Escalades back through the wall heading east, cashing in our clunkers for a 26 horsepower monstrosity that will be the latest production from Government Motors.

We have given up the right to drill for oil in our own country, instead we send our soldiers to the Middle East to fight wars to insure our oil supplies. Why? Geologists believe we have plenty of reserves within our own borders and the ability to bring it to the surface environmentally safer than any other country in the world. We have coal and natural gas reserves that we can use, and do so in an environmentally friendly manner, but politicians won't let us touch them. And nuclear, let's not talk about nuclear. The same politicians say it's fine for Iran, but not OK for southern Ohio.

We have a healthcare system that is the envy of the world, producing more medical breakthroughs than any other country in the world. We have higher survival rates for cancer than countries with socialized medicine and we have emergency rooms that refuse no one, treating anyone that is dumped at their doors, no matter the person's *ability to pay.*

Yet, we're told that system needs to change.

We were told for the past thirty years that, "Trickle Down" economics didn't work under Reagan. Instead, we now have to "bail out" businesses because they're too big to fail. We have to send billions of taxpayer money to banks and big companies so the money will help save our jobs. Apparently we are now practicing "Trickle Up" poverty on the backs of the people, paying for the mistakes of those that can buy off politicians in either party.

We are in a country where the former Financial Services Committee Chairman Barney Frank claimed everyone should own a house. His proposals of giving homes to anyone with a pulse led to the housing crisis. Having a house isn't a right, it's a responsibility. You earn responsibility. Healthcare isn't a right, it's your responsibility. If your job doesn't offer it, you work hard to find one that does. A company that wants quality employees will have to provide quality healthcare to keep them. Now that healthcare is a government mandate, the quality of the service is bound to suffer, not just in healthcare, but in all businesses as the quality of their workers declines.

The government put together the Cash for Clunkers program, funding it with 1 billion dollars to last 4 months. It ran out of money in a week. How soon till the money runs out for healthcare?

It's time to turn the SUVs around and start heading west. It's time to start demanding that our government stop approving laws that they are unwilling to read. It's time to start drilling here to keep our soldiers and our money from going overseas. And it's time that we keep our country from providing us with thirty years of Trabant healthcare.

It's time to stop trying to be like everyone else. We don't have to make excuses for our country. Why do other countries hate us? Because the US has proven itself to be the best damn country in the world. Those that despise us are often in our own country sharing our freedoms while they try to tear them down. They claim that we're an imperial government. Really, an Imperial government? Tell that to the soldiers that shed their blood in Germany twice, in Korea, Vietnam, Iraq twice, and Afghanistan, only to give the land back to the people of that country, only asking for enough land to bury our dead. Imperial my ass. If we were imperial, Germany would have been a state before Hawaii and if you bought a BMW, Mercedes, VW, Audi, or Porsche you'd be buying an American made car.

Liberty, it's time for us to return to American exceptionalism.

Germany can have their luxury cars, we will be the gold standard in everything else. We quite simply need to return to living by our national motto, "In God we Trust." We don't trust in government. Our constitution was written to protect our God given individual freedoms from an oppressive government. If we don't turn back to God and take up our responsibility to serve him, we will become more and more dependent on a government that exploits the workers to benefit the wealthy. In the end, your children's children will only be able to say, "Give me Liberty or give me Debt."

That's my two cents,

Love,
Dad

The Cost of Capitalism

August 4, 2014

Dear Liberty,

For many years we put off vacations so that we could save money. That money eventually bought a cabin in a resort that was near our ancestral farm. A dream your mother and I had before we were even married. It was a risky move to buy the property with no guarantees of money coming in from renters to offset the costs of electric, gas, cable, water, repairs, insurance, management, HOA fees, and taxes that take their cut month after month. Just the purchase of the property ate up virtually all of our savings.

Now that we have the cabin we continue to put off vacations. While others rent the cabin and enjoy hiking, mountain climbing, off-roading, or the zip-line, we come down to the cabin to do repairs. Vacations are not a break from work to reset for the workweek, but rather just more work in a different location. Each time we come to the cabin requires fixing items broken by renters, replacing stolen items, or installing hot tubs, flat panel TVs, and appliances that will improve the experience for future renters.

Time that renters get to spend at Natural Bridge or fishing at the lake are replaced by trips into cities at least 45 minutes away to buy items to make someone else's experience at the cabin better - Someone we don't even know. If that time is not taken, things go into disrepair and eventually the property loses its value to others, their vacation suffers, and soon people will simply stop coming.

We make virtually no money on the cabin. It breaks even at the end of the year once all the costs are taken into consideration. But rather than taking vacations to new places or enjoying ocean cruises, each break we get we simply return to the same little cabin to make repairs.

But somehow, I'm the bad guy. The reason I say that is there is a mentality that has grown in the United States that I didn't earn that. This mindset is pushed out by the media, liberal politicians, and college campuses. It claims that for me to own something means that someone else got cheated out of it.

The truth is someone did get cheated. That someone is me.

52

Rather than enjoying vacations without worry, I spend my off time fixing things that others have broken. Rather than mountain climbing or 4 wheeling, I'm running into town to buy a new door and TV after a burglar forced the back door and made off with a flat panel TV, presumably because I have too much and he didn't have enough.

Why would I waste my limited vacation time to do this? It simply doesn't make any sense. I have no joy in doing the repairs. In fact, rather than getting away from the stress of work I am merely putting new stresses on myself.

This, dear Liberty, is capitalism. This is the right and ability to own property. To claim something as my own and share it with others. I may profit from my choice, or I may fail, but it is mine to do with as I please.

But the liberal/progressive mindset says otherwise. Such a worldview says that in the spirit of justice and fairness everyone should have equal rights to the property and everyone should enjoy in its benefits. Taken to its extreme, this mentality believes the state should own the property and everyone should have equal use of the property as long as they pay tribute to the state.

It does sound fair and each time I enter the crawlspace under the cabin to run a new electrical line or fix a broken water pipe I certainly think about how beneficial it would be for the state to take on this property. They could take on all the work and I could wash my hands of responsibility.

But here in lies the problem. The state takes on neither the work nor the responsibility. They only take on the ownership rights of the property and all its income. They have no personal stake in the cabin. If things get broken or need replaced they have no interest in having them repaired. Everyone will have equal rights to enjoy the property, they simply will be enjoying a cabin that is getting progressively worse.

Unless I have a personal stake in the property I would not waste my time in doing all the work that is necessary to keep it nice for others. The state could have workers make the repairs. The repairs will eventually get done, but with no personal stake, the workers will do the least amount necessary to get by. The worker is merely a cog employed by state with no real interest in what happens to the cabin. At the extreme of socialism, the worker is a person who was told by the state that maintenance work would be his career, not a stepping-stone to something else.

This reveals the dirty truth about socialism. It claims that all the workers are equal and the state has all ownership rights. Everything is fair and no one benefits. But that's not true. The vast majority suffers and only those in power get the true benefits of the wealth. This is no different than feudal Japan or medieval Europe where shoguns and emperors owned the property and the serfs merely worked the land. With no ownership rights, the people do the least work possible, knowing that additional work brings no added benefit to themselves and only additional taxes to the state. The socialists try to claim that capitalism works the same way. What they fail to tell you is that capitalism allows you to pull yourself out of poverty. Socialism keeps you there.

When you understand this, you begin to understand the nature and goals of those in both parties that want to grow government. The Affordable Healthcare Act is an example. It is presented as a benefit to all those that don't have or can't afford insurance. It was for the common man. But who wrote it? Those that needed it, or the insurance companies? After Nancy Pelosi said, "We have to pass the bill to know what's in it," we've come to understand just what it is. It doesn't benefit the people, rather it uses the force of government to require that all people have health insurance or pay a fine. This doesn't benefit the people. It benefits the insurance industry by forcing people by the power of government to buy something that they can't or don't want to pay for. When you understand that, you understand that there is no fairness in what socialism preaches. It only gives more to those that have power and places the costs back on the people.

As for me, I'll take my little cabin in the woods. I suggest you do the same. I'll continue to give up vacations and spend my time making the place more enjoyable for others because I have something I can call my own. Not something forced on me by a government that knows better than I do. Remember all this as you grow up at the cabin, Liberty, because someday it will be yours!

That's my two cents.

Love,
Dad

Is History Repeating Again?

August 7, 2014

Dear Liberty,

"You are an insignificant person!"

Ok, so it's not the caning that Charles Sumner suffered, but when Representative Tom Marino called the Democratic House leaders of 2009-2010 out on Immigration, his words infuriated Nancy Pelosi nearly as much as Preston Brooks 150 years before.

As I described in my letter *The Birth of a Movement*, Senator Sumner, an avid abolitionist, was beaten with a cane by Representative Preston Brooks for his stance against slavery. The beating acted as a harbinger of things to come, leading to the anti-slavery Republican Party, Abraham Lincoln as President, and the beginning of the Civil War. Just as this event magnified the pre-Civil War division in 1856, this uncontrolled and out-of-order outburst by Nancy Pelosi last week is displaying to the world the disunity America is again suffering at this time. This is history in the making, Liberty.

Is this the beginning of another Civil War in America? Only time will tell, but one thing is for sure, it will be less civilized than the War Between the States. At least in that war Americans were grouped by geographical locations and supported by those around them which gave them strength and a coalition. A modern civil war will not only put states against states, but cities against cities, towns against towns, neighbors against neighbors, and even family members against their own. There is no "North" and "South", there is no Mason-Dixon Line, no real boundaries to the divisions.

A positive aspect about this clash is Nancy at least was restrained enough to use just words with her pointy finger and not violence, but how long will that last? It's also incredibly ironic since Senator Ted Cruz was vilified the week before for going and talking to the House Republicans, which was against "Congressional protocol", yet we are not hearing much about Pelosi's complete breach of order. Hey, Nancy, what House rule were you following?

One of the better outcomes that resulted from the Sumner incident was the birth of the Republican Party. Both the Whigs and the Democrats were talking and talking about slavery. This proved to be merely political games that did nothing to solve the problem. The people began to abandon both parties and within years the small Republican Party had won the White House on the prospect of ending slavery.

It all sounds eerily similar to the Tea Party today. The country again finds itself caught in a quagmire of two political parties posturing for political gain, not for the benefit of the people they represent. If God still finds favor with America, the pains we are experiencing now will birth another movement in this county that will return us to the principles of the Constitution. More importantly it will return us to the desire to follow God and his intention for us, to take responsibility for our own actions, and to govern ourselves.

Looking past the disunity, ponder for just a moment what Nancy said to Tom. "You are an insignificant person." This alone shows the whole world how egotistical, arrogant and self-glorifying many of our representatives in Washington have become. Here in lies the growing disease within our government. People like Ms. Pelosi believe they are better than you, know better than you and believe they have the right to control you. This was EXACTLY what the Founding Fathers not only warned against but designed the Constitution and the Bill of Rights to prevent. Unfortunately, this mindset has infected both parties and is what plain, simple Americans want to rid our government of. Politicians beat their chests and proudly proclaim, "I've been in the Congress for 40 years..." Sir, that is nothing to brag about. It's an indictment.

The Founding Fathers intended that good, honest people should serve their country for a few years and then return to their lives making way for others to do their turn. Politics was never meant to be a profession, never meant to make people rich, and never, ever intended to give so few so much control. I'm sure most politicians go to Washington with the desire to do good, but the money, the benefits and mostly the power becomes so intoxicating, it overwhelms one's desire to represent the people and makes one want to rule the people. This small grammatical difference makes a huge difference mentally.

Liberty, I have no idea what America and this world will look like when you are actually old enough to read and understand this letter and the others I am writing you. I pray it is a much better place still striving for liberty and freedom for all. Like the time of the Sumner attack when no one could have predicted for certain that a physical war was on the horizon, I have no idea what will happen tomorrow. I promise to you right now though, Liberty, that I will do everything I can to educate people, mend fences and learn to disagree while still standing on my principles. I promise that your father and I will do everything we can to prevent a repeat of the Civil War and we promise to do everything we can to leave you a better country than we found.

I pray you look back on this letter and are able to say, "Thank you, Mom and Dad. You did it." and not "You saw what was happening. Why didn't you save my freedoms?" Either way, the fight does not end with us, Liberty. The torch will eventually be passed to you. You must speak out for your children's freedom as Sumner spoke out for freedom for the slaves. And then you must pass the torch again. This is a fight that will be fought until Christ returns and declares ultimate and eternal freedom. Stay strong, stay educated, and stay passionate, holding your Bible high in one hand and the Constitution in the other.

That's my 2 cents.

Love,
Mom

Independence: It's In Our DNA

August 13, 2014

Dear Liberty,

As you grabbed your toothbrush from my hand and said, "Let me, mommy", I began to realize how you have been striving from the beginning to have your freedom and independence. You started pushing yourself up on me and strengthening your legs at just a few months old. You were eager to start feeding yourself and worked hard to crawl and then walk. Your verbal skills are developing so well you'll probably have our own talk show by this time next year. But most interesting is your favorite phrase for some time now, "Let Liberty do it".

Independence and self-reliance is in our blood, Liberty. It is in all living DNA. It is fascinating to me that people who claim to be evolutionists argue and demand that animals not be kept in captivity. They should be left alone in the wild to live as they were meant to be, understanding that animals learn to take care of themselves from extremely early ages. Even signs at our local park warn:

> *Feeding Wildlife Can Be Harmful*
> *Feeding Can Cause:*
> *Dependency on people for food.*
> *Loss of survival instincts.*

Yet, many of these same people insist that there are large parts of the human population that must be taken care of by the few that are fortunate enough to be successful. If we evolved from animals, wouldn't it be consistent that humans should be able to take care of themselves, too, especially since evolution is a process of becoming better, not weaker? That giving people handout after handout will make them dependent? And those who are trying to increase their survival skills are called "extreme", "crazy" and "preppers" as if they were backwoods hicks and not as brilliant as the elitists who have everything done for them. Basically, we are supposed to believe that the most intelligent species on earth is the least self-reliant.

So ask yourself, does the raccoon ask where she can build her nest or does she do what is best for her and her family? Does the mare keep her colt down or does she gentle nudge him until he is standing and then walking shortly after birth? Does the robin sit in her nest waiting for *someone to find her worms or does she provide for her own? Does the stingray refrain from using his stinger because his opponent is not equally equipped, or does he defend himself as he sees necessary? Just as God designed the birds of the air, the fish in the sea and the creatures of the land to provide for themselves, He planted that same desire and instinct in man to not be beholden to anyone. Our only King is Christ.*

Liberty, God gave each of us not only the ability but the yearning to take care of ourselves. Our Founding Fathers understood this and made it the backbone of our country's founding documents. It was a brand new concept as never before had people had the right and the responsibility to govern themselves.

This was the only country where one could move up or down the social status ladder by their own effort and hard work or lack there of. A person was no longer born into a position of poverty or wealth where they were guaranteed to remain for life. They had the freedom to lift themselves out of the slums, get an education, and pursue whatever career or dream they desired. No King, no dictator, no emperor putting the shackles of predetermined destiny around ones ankles with a future no better than their ancestors before them. Likewise, no one was guaranteed a high social or political position just because of their parent's status. This is, until now.

America has been invaded by the ideology of communism/socialism/progressivism, which insists people need to be controlled and ruled. The best way to do that is to make them dependent, which goes against the basic fibers of our being. The ruling class, politicians and the elites are actively trying to force America into a hierarchal society keeping them in power and the people their servants and impoverished. When I was a teacher 15 years ago, I had students who were 3rd and 4th generation welfare recipients. Many already had babies, resigning themselves to lives of poverty for them and their children by age 16.

On the other side, we have people today believing Hillary Clinton or Michelle Obama should be president. Why? Just because their husbands were? I've even heard some mention Chelsea Clinton should be in line for it too. It's just as bad on the Republican side. The GOP elites are actually pushing a third Bush for office with other little Bushes waiting in the wings. No more! We are not a monarchy.

With every new welfare recipient, with every new government food card and with every new illegal immigrant that signs up for ObamaCare, we are one step closer to a majority of dependents in this country that dangerously outweigh the producers. They will have no choice but to vote in those who promise to keep the money coming thus virtually securing permanent political power for anyone willing to give the country away.

As Winston Churchill once said, "You can always count on Americans to do the right thing - after they've tried everything else." Though progressivism and socialism started creeping in over 100 years ago, the biggest push came with the radicals of the 60's. Those extremists are now in charge of our country. We are trying socialism. We are trying communism. We are trying progressivism. We've tried "everything else." It doesn't work. Liberty, let's pray Prime Minister Churchill was right and your fellow countrymen are on the brink of doing the right thing.

That's my 2 cents.

Love,
Mom

Just The Facts, Ma'am

August 20, 2014

Dear Liberty,

    Fact - Michael Brown and his friend robbed a store, stole cigarillos, and Michael assaulted the worker.

    Fact - Michael Brown was walking down the middle of the street with his friend after the robbery.

    Fact - 10 minutes later an officer saw Michael and his friend and asked them to get off the street.

    Fact - The officer may have been unaware that Michael Brown had just robbed a store.

    Fact - However, Michael was perfectly aware that he had just robbed the store by assaulting the employee.

    Fact - The officer's face is fractured, indicating a struggle.

    Fact - Two autopsy reports show that the bullets entered Michael from the front.

    Fact - Autopsy report also shows marijuana in Michael's system.

    Fact - Over 12 witnesses have now corroborate the story that Michael Brown pushed the officer into his cruiser, a scuffle over the officer's gun ensued, causing a shot to be fired. Michael then got out of cruiser and began to run. When the cop followed him Michael turned around and charged the officer.

    Liberty, these are the facts that are finally coming out regarding the recent shooting of a young man by a police officer in Ferguson, Missouri. Unfortunately no one in the mainstream media cared to wait even a second to find the facts. Instead they started making their own assumptions, their own conclusions, their own narrative, and putting the blame on the cop. All we were told was a young, unarmed black man was walking down the street from his grandma's house back to his apartment when a cop pulled up and started harassing him and his friend. The young men raised their hands when the officer approached, but the officer shot Michael in the back anyway. As a result of this disinformation we have another set of facts.

    Fact - People are looting local stores and setting some on fire claiming they are angry.

    Fact - Protesters threw Molotov cocktails at officers (again, which the media failed to report) and officers had to tear gas the protesters (which the media vigorously reported)

    Fact - The agitators in the uproar are largely coming from Oakland, California, including but not limited to the New Black

Panthers, Communists and the Justice Department.

Fact - The peaceful protesters of Ferguson do not want the violence and are telling the agitators to go home.

We are being told again and again how common it is that cops are shooting innocent, young black men for no reason. But what no one is asking is if this really were so common, why don't we hear about it more often? If this happens regularly all over the country, shouldn't there be stories like this in the news every week? This event is being compared to the Rodney King incident in LA. That incident occurred 20 years ago. Is that what they mean by common?

Once again a minority group is being used to promote a lie and a radical agenda. These people have been made to believe, without waiting for any evidence or facts, that an officer decided to just go out one Saturday afternoon and shoot a black man. If that's true, why wasn't his companion, who has since changed his story, also shot? As the truth is coming out bit by bit, the same agitators causing the unrest are doing everything they can to spin that truth to keep their pawns angry, continue the chaos and give themselves power.

Liberty, incidents like this are going to affect you more than most by the simple fact that your dad is a cop. The truth is most people are just trying to live their lives and not bother anyone. The people your dad deals with daily are the people that say they don't trust the police, but are the first to call the police to solve their problems. Despite that, your father always treats people with respect, even those that have committed a crime. However, if someone gets aggressive with him he is expected by society to use enough force to stop the threat. That might entail shooting someone. Not because of his beliefs, or the race of the person, but based solely on the offender's actions.

I am sure without a doubt that there are many, many very concerned people in Ferguson who want to know what really happened with Michael Brown. Unfortunately there are those who see this as an opportunity for political gain. What they fail to realize is that when the country and the world see the young, ignorant men and women looting in the streets using this man's death as an excuse for theft and violence, they are hurting their cause more than they will ever help it.

Some have even been interviewed on the news and claim they are taking what they deserve. How do they deserve a TV because the young man was killed? What is even more telling is while Al Sharpton is in Ferguson talking about how unacceptable and horrible this is that another young black man was taken, there were about 40 shootings in Chicago alone this weekend resulting in at least five dead young black people. If he was that concerned about the death of young African

Americans, he would be in Chicago every day preaching to those people. But he is not. He is a race baiter, looking only to profit from circumstances. The only black man that has benefitted from his presence on the national scene the past 25 years is Al Sharpton.

Liberty, you cannot allow your emotions to overpower your intellect. That does not mean that you should not be concerned for people, that you should not stand up for people, or that you should not try to change wrongs when you can. But you cannot let someone manipulate those feelings into anger and violence because they have another agenda. It is up to you to learn the facts, know the facts, and wait for the facts before you make a judgment.

I am not saying at this point that the cop was guilty or innocent. But as our Founding Fathers wrote, people are presumed innocent until proven guilty. Which goes for Michael Brown as well. Referring to the facts stated above, though, the incident is shaping out to look like a completely different story than what we were originally told at the beginning.

The best weapon you have is your mind. Once you stop using it and blindly follow a voice, any voice, without exercising your responsibility to do your own research, then you have handed over your liberty and freedom to someone else. Who, by the way, will joyfully take it from you.

That's my 2 cents.

Love,
Mom

Family Feud

August 27, 2014

Dear Liberty,

Benjamin Netanyahu, Israel's Prime Minister, recently stated, "We [Israel] use missiles to protect our people, they [Hamas] use people to protect their missiles."

The terrorists, knowing the liberal, anti-Semitic media will turn a blind eye, launch their missiles from hospitals, schools, private homes and playgrounds confident that Israel will retaliate. Once the inevitable damage happens to the Palestinians, photographs of the injured and killed are quickly circulated as propaganda against the Jews. That's when the media and liberal politicians launch their own assault against Israel, never publicizing the initial attack from Hamas. Israel's response is highly reported as brutality from the Jews on the Arabs, thus poisoning the opinion of Israel in the minds of citizens all over the world. There are even incidents where Hamas' own weapons cause the death and destruction, but they still blame Israel.

Why? Why is there such hatred of the tiny area about the size of New Jersey known as Israel by Arabs that overwhelmingly surround them of the Middle East? And can it be solved by political opportunist that continually fail at peace since 1948? Is it just because they want that little piece of land?

This is not a new hatred that developed when Israel was recognized as a country by the UN in 1948. It's essentially a family squabble over an inheritance that goes back to the first book of the Bible. It can be traced back to the Father of Judaism, Christianity, and Islam. It all goes back to Abraham.

God guaranteed Abraham that He would not only bless him and Sarah with descendants more numerous than the stars in the sky despite their advanced ages, His real covenant was humanity's promised Savior would be one of those children. In a moment of impatience and weak faith, Sarah sinned trying to "help" God by offering Hagar, a servant, to Abraham. Abraham sinned by accepting Sarah's idea and taking Hagar as a mate. A child was produced, Abraham's first, named Ishmael. Before the baby was even born, tensions of jealousy and pride arose between Sarah and Hagar, a result of their sin of unfaithfulness in God's promise that we still suffer from today. Fearful of her mistress' anger, Hagar ran away but was visited and comforted by an angel of God who promised she would be protected, so she returned to Abraham's camp.

Ishmael was loved and nurtured by his father into his teen years before God decided it was time to fulfill his promise to Abraham and Sarah. After the birth of Isaac, though Ishmael was raised in the faith of his father, he rejected God's promise by mocking his half brother. Sarah, who once offered Hagar to her husband, now demanded that same woman and her son be banished from the tribe fearing Ishmael would threaten the inheritance God promised Isaac. Heartbroken at the loss of his son, God comforted both Abraham and Hagar by reminding them of His assurance of a great nation through Ishmael, which came true through the Arab people.

Over the years, Ishmael and his descendants are referenced in the Old Testament, both settling and intermarrying with Isaac's descendants. Ishmael stood with his brother Isaac when their father died and they buried him together as siblings. Joseph, Isaac's grandson, was sold into slavery by his brothers to Ishmaelites. On the day of Pentecost, one of the tongues, or languages, spoken was Arabic, so God definitely did not withhold His promise of salvation from Ishmael and his descendants. So what changed?

Muhammad, a descendant of Ishmael, believed his ancestor was a prophet and the rightful heir of God's promise to Abraham, not Isaac. The most holy place for Muslims is Mecca, the traditional Muslim residence of Ishmael after his exile as well as Muhammad's birthplace. It homes the Kaaba, a square stone building supposedly built by Abraham on a visit to see Ishmael at Mecca.

During a 6-month journey of prayer and self-introspection, Muhammad claims he was visited by the angel Gabriel who gave him the words for the Quran. Upon his return he began preaching his new religion. After having to flee to Medina with his followers and frustrated that many were not converting, Muhammad began instructing his followers that if people refused to change, it not only pleased God but he commanded that they murder the infidels. In fact, Islam preaches that if a Muslim dies for his faith while killing unbelievers, he will be greatly rewarded and their family would be held in high esteem.

This goal could not be more evident than by the current events happening in Iraq under ISIS control right now. The Islamic extremists are not only killing Christians and other infidels in the towns they are overrunning, they are beheading their victims and placing the heads on fence pikes along the road. In fact, these radical Muslims are so extreme they will kill other Muslims, whether it be Sunnis vs. Shi'ites, or *simply if they do not subscribe to the fanaticism of Islam and dare to dream of liberty and freedom instead of the shackles of Sharia Law. Laws which, among other things, reduce the worth of a woman to that of mere property and allow corporal punishment at the whim of men instead of judges and juries.*

Jews, Christians and Muslims all believe in a monotheist, creationist God. All believe Abraham existed and was favored by God. All believe that Abraham had 2 sons, Ishmael and Isaac, and all believe the Torah is God's law and guide for our lives. At this point one path preaches peace and one path preaches war. But even while Palestinians have it written in their charters that their goal is to eradicate every Jew off the face of the earth, Barack Obama rationalizes it is reasonable to tell Israel to "show restraint" while extremists in the Gaza Strip continuously attack their innocent women and children.

I want to believe that there are moderate, cordial Muslims that do not endorse this radical violence, but when I watch video of terrorists launching missiles from playgrounds and all the surrounding citizens are cheering knowing it's mission is to destroy Israeli people, I have to question the idea of peaceful Islamists. Citizens that cheer when captured infidels are murdered and dragged through the streets or celebrate when things like September 11, 2001 happens to America. What religion allows the beheading of James Foley, an American photojournalist, and defends themselves as peaceful?

Secretary of State Kerry tried to broker a cease-fire with some sort of compromising conditions. One thing he did do is bring all parties together to laugh at and mock his ridiculous treaty. The truth is Israel would love to end the fighting but how do you compromise with someone who wants to murder your entire race? Agree to allow the extremists to kill just half of the Jews? Once that's achieved, would they again demand to kill another half? Even though there is a cease-fire called at this time, it won't be long before Hamas strikes again.

Jesus instructed his disciples to spread the Good News to every corner of the world. If a town rejected their message, the disciples were directed to "wipe the dust from their feet" and move to the next city leaving the people to suffer the judgment of God. Muhammad also instructed his followers to spread their faith across the world, but Muhammad required believers to take judgment upon themselves when one did not convert. How does a rational person find compromise in these two viewpoints? The same tensions continue today that existed between Sarah and Hagar all those years ago, but which path has shown to be more peaceful? Which religion is more tolerant? Which one do you think is more pleasing to God? That being said, Muslims do not hate Jews as a religion per se, they despise Jews as a nation calling them pigs and producing children's shows promoting the hatred and murder of the Israeli people.

Muslims will adamantly reject that their hatred of Israel boils down to birthright yet they have the same feud within their own faith. When Muhammad died, leadership of the Islam nation was expected to fall to one of two followers: Ali, Muhammad's cousin and son-in-law, or Omar, a Muhammad general. Omar resolved the debate by killing Ali. Sunnis, followers of Omar and 90% of Muslims, hate, fight and kill Shi'ites, followers of Ali, and vice versa, just like they would any other infidel.

This was all talked about 2000 years before Muhammad when Moses wrote "The Book", which even Muhammad supported as stated above. When Hagar left the first time, the angel of the Lord told her, "He [Ishmael] shall be a wild ass among man; his hand shall be against every man, and every man's hand against him; and he shall dwell over against all his brethren." (Genesis 16:12) In other words, Ishmael will live in opposition to all. A trait Muhammad possessed as well as he believed in complete domination of the world in the Islamic faith. Even Paul described the relationship and conflict between Sarah's offspring, the son of promise to a free woman and Hagar's, the son of flesh to a slave woman, approximately 600 years before Muhammad was inspired to write the Quran.

Liberty, I am writing you this letter so you know the truth because it is being deliberately distorted in our modern history books. You have to always seek out the truth, even if it means finding out facts that you don't want to know. As the Bible says, "The truth shall set you free." Though it is referring to the Good News of Jesus Christ, the phrase does ring true in a broader sense. If you know the truth, not only will you be empowered to retain your liberty, you can pass that power on to others so they can keep theirs. Even Jefferson understood the importance of knowing and understanding the truth, which is why he recommended everyone read the Quran. Not to be converted to Islam, but to understand what we are actually fighting against. And Liberty, the information in this letter is only the tip of the iceberg.

That's my 2 cents.

Love,
Mom

The Man Who Refused To Be King

September 3, 2014

Dear Liberty,

As we enter the mid-term election season, it seems like there is more talk about the 2016 Presidential election than the current 2014 elections. Tongues are also frantically beginning to wag as to who will succeed Obama. But why do we limit our presidents to 2 terms in office?

About 458 B.C. Rome was attacked by the Aequi. At a critical moment, the Roman Senate turned to Cincinnatus for help. They elected him dictator for a 6-month period, informing him while he was tending his 4-acre farm. Honoring this appointment, Cincinnatus left his plow in the field, his wife in the house and traveled to Rome to assume his position. After choosing his second in command, Tarquitius, and ordering all men of military age to service, he engaged in fighting against the Aequi. He personally led the infantry while Tarquitius commanded the cavalry. Surprised by the double attack, the Aequi were easily defeated and were soon begging for mercy from the newly elected dictator. Showing compassion, Cincinnatus spared the lives of the remaining enemy soldiers under the condition that they surrender their leader. With the war over, Cincinnatus sent his army home, resigned his position, and returned to his family and farm. How long was he dictator? Fifteen days. Not a day longer than necessary.

Because of the selflessness, integrity, and uniqueness of the actions of Cincinnatus, he has been revered and respected by people to this day. He was taught about in schools and written about in poetry even at the time of America's founding some 2200 years later. He also inspired other great leaders, such as George Washington, often referred to in his day as the American Cincinnatus. Though it took a little more than 15 days, after being called out of retirement on his farm by his country to command the Continental Army, Washington was led by nothing less than duty and responsibility to the cause of freedom.

While so many before him took the torch they were given and ruled for their lifetime or until their defeat, Washington, like Cincinnatus, viewed military and service as it was intended to be, service. He slept in the freezing cold at Valley Forge along with his men and he rallied his troops from the front on top of his horse, often drawing the fire of the enemy. Washington was never one to demand anymore from someone that he was not willing to do himself. And he never expected to be pampered or protected like royalty.

Upon hearing that Washington would return to his farm after he won independence for America, King George III stated, "If he does that, he will be the greatest man in the world." The notion of giving up power was actually a very rare concept until America. Dictatorships, monarchies, emperorships, all these governments revolve around political power being for life and then passed from generation to generation. Only bloodshed and war unseated a ruler. That is until America. That is until George Washington.

It was not long after the end of the Revolutionary War until Washington was called away from his farm again by his country, this time to participate in the Constitutional Convention of 1787 to which he was unanimously voted president of the meeting. His ethics, his morals, and the way he led his life was not only the perfect example of American Exceptionalism, it is a personal standard a vast majority are still trying to live up to today. (see God's Divine Providence-Vol.3) Washington was not loved and adored because he could give good speeches or he promised voters the moon. He was respected and admired because of his humility, his faithfulness to God and country (in that order), and his trustworthiness. Who better to be the first person to be given the powerful position of Presidency than someone who does not live for power. At the conclusion of his second term, Washington informed the citizens that he would not seek a third. This was the second time Washington walked away from absolute power, authority and entitlement. He spent years defeating a monarchy. Why would he then establish one here?

Our Constitution did not originally put a limit on the number of terms the President could serve in office. It only defined a single term as 4 years. Washington knew the amazing importance of his position and how his actions would shape that office for decades to come. It would have been so easy to live out the rest of his life as President of the United States. There is no doubt he would have won election after election.

But, contrary to what the progressive movement is trying to ignore, Washington was a Godly man. Because of this he was self-disciplined and believed if citizens followed God and his commands then they would be more than capable of governing themselves. It was not meant for one man to rule over the people but for the people to rule themselves. This meant a real change in leadership on a regular basis to which Washington led by example.

Out of respect for the "Father of Our Country" and following his model, none of the next 30 presidents that held a second term received a third. It was not until Democrat Franklin D. Roosevelt that any president was granted an extended tenure. After his death at the beginning of his 4th term, Congress quickly passed an amendment that restored the unwritten precedent set by Washington to the Office of the President limiting the number of terms served to 2.

In 1783 the military preservation organization, called the Society of the Cincinnati, was formed with the motto Omnia reliquit servare rempublicam ("He relinquished everything to save the Republic") emphasizing the selfless service of the military. The Society had three goals: "To preserve the rights so dearly won; to promote the continuing union of the states; and to assist members in need, their widows, and their orphans." It was no surprise that General George Washington was elected their first president. A few years later a small village in Southwest Ohio borrowed the Society's name and became the thriving city of Cincinnati.

Liberty, since you were born and are being raised in Cincinnati, my hope is that from now on, every time you write or see your city name, you remember the story of Cincinnatus and more relevantly Washington. I want you to remember the true meaning of military and public service and the example these two men have given us.

So whenever a politician pompously proclaims that he has been in office 40 years, you have the wisdom to know that is actually a mark of disgrace, not a badge of honor. Government was never meant to be saturated with career politicians who exempt themselves from the laws they write and broker deals that make them rich. It was supposed to be run by hardworking farmers, miners, engineers, shop owners, ranchers, architects, doctors, entrepreneurs, inventors, educators, and yes, even clergy, bankers and lawyers, who have more love for their land, trade, and fellow citizens than power and authority.

That's my 2 cents.

Love,
Mom

Never Forget

September 11, 2014

Dear Liberty,

    The talking points are out and the left is falling in line as ordered. Not only has the president pushed numerous times that climate change is our greatest crisis, Secretary of State John Kerry also recently said that Biblically we are suppose to protect the Muslims from global warming.

    The Middle East is on fire but not due to global warming. America's economy is in the tank, Russia is on the verge of overtaking Ukraine, race riots are flaring up in Ferguson, Missouri, terrorists and other illegals are flooding over our border and global warming is our greatest threat? Either these people are incredibly clueless or extremely dangerous.

    In 2007, Al Gore told the world that the Arctic ice caps were melting so fast they'd be gone in 7 years which is...well, now. Reality is the Arctic ice caps are having a surge in growth at this time, increasing at unforeseen rates. Not only is global warming proving to be not as bad as predicted, those predictions are proving to be the total opposite of reality. Funny how we are suppose to hold science as the end all and be all, unless the results completely decimate the left's agenda. Instead of looking at the facts and admitting their theories were wrong, they are desperately holding on to what they want to be true and trying hopelessly to find reasons to explain the cause of the discrepancy. The earth hasn't warmed in 18 years, Liberty, yet they still believe their unreliable computer models are the truth and the evidence of the actual weather is not reality.

    To top his speech off, Kerry said the Muslim religion is a peaceful religion. Well, I'll be sure to tell the two journalists who were just beheaded by ISIS, the four Americans that were murdered in Benghazi on September 11, 2012 as well as the 3000 people who were massacred on September 11, 2001. Many people want to bury the truth about September 11th so they can make idiotic claims that climate change is our biggest threat. With this being the anniversary of the 9-11 attack I think it is important, Liberty, for you to be told what really happened that day. Let me give you some of the facts and events of that day so you can decide what is more threatening.

    The morning of September 11th we were on our way home from

visiting relatives in Houston, Texas, and were about to start our second day of driving. I turned on the TV to see what was on while we got ready to leave, mostly intent on checking out the weather. I turned on the TV to an image of the 1st World Trade Center tower falling, followed shortly by the 2nd tower. I just sunk onto the bed with my mouth open trying to call for your daddy. We had about 8 hours to go and it was the longest 8 hours I've ever had in the car. We barely talked. We listened all day to the radio commentators reviewing the latest news. We, like the rest of the country, were trying desperately to figure out what was happening.

We heard facts about the 58,000 people the World Trade Center towers employed. The speculations of how many flights were hijacked. The reports of the other planes going down in Washington D.C. and Pennsylvania. The plans for vigils at churches all across America. How many planes did the terrorists have? How many places were going to be hit? Would this be happening all day? What could we do?

Soon the facts began to reveal themselves. Nineteen young men, mostly from Saudi Arabia but all affiliated with al-Qaeda, came to America with destruction on their minds and evil in their souls. A few attended flight school, while most were to simply act as "muscle" to overpower the crewmembers and passengers. They spent a few months in the states making their final plans as to which day, which flights and which targets. The chosen flights were all long distance flights, meaning the tanks were full of aviation fuel to cause the most damage and death. They seized the planes with box cutters and plastic knives and forced their way into the cockpits. Two of the planes headed for the World Trade Center twin towers, one plane headed for the Pentagon and the fourth plane never made it to its destination. Your aunt that lives in the area was working in her garden and saw a low-flying plane that morning, realizing later that she witnessed the doomed flight moments before it crashed.

The two planes that went to the World Trade Center were used as manned missiles to attack each tower. The passengers on both planes were killed instantly along with hundreds in the towers upon impact. The planes did explode, igniting intense fires and causing hundreds of gallons of jet fuel to pour down the framework only to escalate the fires. The fires were so hot people actually jumped out of the 110 story buildings to escape the horrific inferno. At the same time, fire fighters and police officers put aside their own lives, running into the buildings

to rescue whoever they could. Most didn't make it.

I remember seeing the video of when the towers fell and the dust and debris that rolled through the streets of New York City. It only took seconds for the streets to become black as night due to the dust and rubble. People were running frantically down the streets diving into shops trying to avoid being overrun with dust. Can you imaging the fear on that day?

The airliner that was used to strike the Pentagon was flying so low and slow that people on the ground could see the faces of the passengers before they hit the building. Can you imagine the terror those people must have felt knowing their imminent fate?

The last plane's final destination is still not known, but we do know it was heading to Washington D.C. It is speculated that the intended target was either the Capital Building or the White House. Passengers aboard Flight 93 contacted family members via cell phones and said they were hijacked, only to learn of the three other crashed planes. The brave patriots aboard Flight 93 harnessed the courage to take back the plane. The last thing heard from the passengers was, "Let's roll." The terrorists responded by crashing the plane in Pennsylvania while shouting, "Allahu Akbar!", the Islamic phrase used by Islamists as they slaughter infidels.

Liberty, you might be wondering why I am writing this letter. There are a few reasons. One is because there are too many people these days trying to shield Americans from the evil that exists in this world. Some do it because they honestly think they are protecting the people. Others do it so they can make statements like, "Islam is a peaceful religion" to further their own agenda.

If we do not continue to study the past and heed the warning signs of former events then history will inevitably repeat itself. For example, on February 26, 1993 the World Trade Center was attacked with a car bomb in the parking garage. There was damage, but loss of life was minimal. The administration at the time, under President Bill Clinton, refused to look at this as a terrorist attack, prosecuting those involved as simple criminals rather than the terrorists they were. They were trained by al-Qaeda with ties to Osama Bin Laden, the mastermind of the 9-11 attack. America was attacked several more times overseas but the administration turned a blind eye, continuing to believe there was no threat even though the terrorists warned they were coming.

We are back to that same mentality today. The current administration warns of the imminent threat of global warming, while Muslims are executing Christians at will in Egypt, Iraq, and other Islamic states, beheading journalists, and terrorizing Israel. They are forcing Sharia Law in Germany and telling America "We'll see you in New York." Just last week it was reported that there are eleven missing airliners from Libya with a picture recently surfacing of terrorists with one of the aircraft.

With this information, Liberty, please ask yourself, are the Islamic Extremists who are forcing a caliphate a pretty important threat, or is the left correct that the philosophy of global warming, which is constantly being disproved and shown as inaccurate, our biggest challenge? Don't trust politicians. Trust your own reason, Liberty.

While Muslims on the other side of the world celebrated the death and destruction on September 11th, Christians did take comfort that day in the fact that considering how many people could have perished in the demolition of the Twin Towers, most were able to escape the burning tombs. Of all the sides and sections the plane could have entered the Pentagon, it hit at a spot that was actually relatively unoccupied due to recent reconstruction. We don't know where the fourth plane would have hit, but how many lives were saved due to the courage and unselfish sacrifice of the passengers of that plane? As the world burns, Liberty, we must hold to the promise that God is in control. He does not promise there will be no trials, tribulations or evil but through the blood of His son Jesus Christ we have already achieved victory.

That's my 2 cents.

Love,
Mom

September 18, 2014

Dear Liberty,

There is an incredible push in America demanding everyone accept same sex marriage whether they agree with it or not. An overwhelming number of states, including the ultra-liberal California, have voted to honor the traditional definition of marriage. However, agenda driven judges are overturning these laws created by the people on a regular basis, which completely ignores the rights of the people to govern themselves.

The majority of Americans, like myself, are not trying to deprive same sex couples of anything. We are merely following the laws of God. We are told in the beginning, God created Adam, and then Eve from him, "That is why a man leaves his father and mother and is united to his wife, and they become one flesh." (Genesis 2:24)

God went further in the 4th Commandment instructing us to "Honor your father and your mother, that your days may be long in the land that the LORD your God is giving you." It is obvious God expected a child to have a mother and father, because the strength of the family unit supports itself. If that unit is broken down, it increases the chances that the individuals will not turn their reliance on each other, but on the government.

The true biblical reason for marriage is to reveal to us that Christ is the groom and his church is his bride. In Jesus' time, the marriage promise began when a man and woman were engaged. The groom would leave the bride with her family and go to prepare a house for the couple. The bride waited for him, remaining faithful and pure. Upon the groom's return he would officially marry his bride and take her to their new home. This is what Christ meant when he told his disciples that he was going away "to prepare a place for them," and would soon return for them.

Heaven is that place, our eternal home, and Jesus will come again to collect believers to take back to Paradise. Our pastor reiterated this comparison the night of our wedding rehearsal, emphasizing that your daddy was representing Christ on our wedding day. I, while wearing white to show my innocence and purity, represented the church. This analogy made our wedding vows and ceremony so much more *meaningful, important, and eloquent. This is why Christians cannot, in good conscience, celebrate the overt defiance of this significant institution by saying gay marriage is fine with God.*

Many people do not believe in all of this mumbo jumbo. To them the Bible is nothing more than silly stories. They argue that we should be more accepting and tolerant towards others. Yet they refuse to accept or tolerate my faith, my beliefs and my traditions? I understand the desire of a homosexual person to want to bond and share their life with the person they love. They want the right to visit their loved one in the hospital, have legal parental rights, or have the same health and death benefits as a married couple. I'm fine with that. Those are legal issues. That's why I support civil unions that give gays and lesbians these important benefits. What I object to is this relentless attack on the sanctity of marriage, which was instituted by God, not by government.

But the truth is, the gay marriage movement isn't about gay rights at all, but rather the destruction of traditional marriage. Masha Gessen, a leader in the gay marriage movement, gave a speech in 2012 admitting this was not about gay marriage, but about breaking up the traditional family and eradicating marriage altogether.

That being said, I cannot ignore God's statements regarding homosexuality. God loves all His children. He wants every one of them to live in eternity with Him. But to do that one must first accept Christ as their Lord and Savior and repent from sinful desires. If you continue in purposeful sinning, you are rejecting the Word of the LORD. Repentance is your response to your natural sins. Many excuse homosexual behavior by stating, "I'm born this way." Would that be an acceptable excuse for a murderer, a thief, a rapist, a child molester? If you do not repent, you cannot be forgiven. If you are not forgiven, you cannot receive the benefits of Christ covering those sins for you. He died for everyone's sins, but if you do not repent then you are rejecting the blessing of that forgiveness.

As a Christian we are faced today with the pressure from media, Hollywood, politicians, and peers to keep our mouths shut and not only accept sinful living but to celebrate it. We are told if we don't we are not loving people. But how is it loving to allow someone to condemn themselves to Hell just so they don't have to feel uncomfortable here on Earth? Many churches are accepting practicing homosexuals in their folds, and even in their pulpits, telling their congregation that God is ok with it. If they are truly following the words of God then these verses should be burning in their hearts:

Leviticus 18:22 - *"Do not practice homosexuality, having sex with another man as with a woman. It is a detestable sin."*

Leviticus 20:13 - *"If a man practices homosexuality, having sex with another man as with a woman, both men have committed a detestable act. They must both be put to death, for they are guilty of a capital offense."*

Romans 1:24-27 - *"So God abandoned them to do whatever shameful things their hearts desired. As a result, they did vile and degrading things with each other's bodies. They traded the truth about God for a lie. So they worshiped and served the things God created instead of the Creator himself, who is worthy of eternal praise! Amen. That is why God abandoned them to their shameful desires. Even the women turned against the natural way to have sex and instead indulged in sex with each other. And the men, instead of having normal sexual relations with women, burned with lust for each other. Men did shameful things with other men, and as a result of this sin, they suffered within themselves the penalty they deserved."*

For those that argue that the Bible was written for a different time, perhaps you should read the Romans' passage again. It sounds as if Paul was writing an editorial in the newspaper today.

But it's important to realize that it's not just homosexuality that God condemns, it is all sexual sin. He puts these sins on the same level as lying, cheating, stealing, murder, abuse, coveting, idol worship, and the like. God judges a heterosexual couple living together outside of marriage the same way he judges a homosexual couple. Both acts are jeopardizing the possibility of obtaining eternal life. A man who preys on women is just as detested as the man who preys on other men.

1 Corinthians 6:9-11 - *"Don't you realize that those who do wrong will not inherit the Kingdom of God? Don't fool yourselves. Those who indulge in sexual sin, or who worship idols, or commit adultery, or are male prostitutes, or practice homosexuality, or are thieves, or greedy people, or drunkards, or are abusive, or cheat people-none of these will inherit the Kingdom of God. Some of you were once like that. But you were cleansed; you were made holy; you were made right with God by calling on the name of the Lord Jesus Christ and by the Spirit of our God."*

Matthew 15:18-20 - *"But the things that come out of the mouth come from the heart, and these make a man unclean. For out of the heart come evil thoughts, murder, adultery, sexual immorality, theft, false testimony, slander. These are what make a man unclean; but eating with unwashed hands does not make him unclean."*

Galatians 5:19-23 - *"When you follow the desires of your sinful* *nature, the results are very clear: sexual immorality, impurity, lustful pleasures, idolatry, sorcery, hostility, quarreling, jealousy, outbursts of anger, selfish ambition, dissension, division, envy, drunkenness, wild parties, and other sins like these. Let me tell you again, as I have before, that anyone living that sort of life will not inherit the Kingdom of God. But the Holy Spirit produces this kind of fruit in our lives: love, joy, peace, patience, kindness, goodness, faithfulness, gentleness, and self-control. There is no law against these things!"*

These are only just a few of the verses discussing the issue. Some try to argue that Jesus would love and accept homosexuals anyway. I agree. He definitely loves them, but because He loves them He would not overlook their behavior. When he saved the adulteress from stoning he did not tell her to continue her sinful life. He told her, "Go and sin no more."

But Christ also spoke on marriage, making it clear that as God He defined marriage as:

Mark 10:6-9 - *(Jesus said) "But at the beginning of creation God 'made them male and female'. For this reason a man will leave his father and mother and be united to his wife, and the two will become one flesh. So they are no longer two, but one flesh. Therefore what God has joined together, let no one separate."*

He specifically noted God made male and female. They should be united and no one should separate them. This does not mean that we hate those who choose not to follow this command, but Christians deserve the right to hold this belief, live by this belief, and not be forced to defy this belief.

There used to be a sign in many businesses saying, "We reserve the right to refuse service to anyone." Today, however, we are hearing more and more reports of homosexuals suing businesses because the Christian owners refused to go against their religious freedoms and recognize a gay wedding. If someone didn't want to provide a service for my wedding, why would I sue them for it? Why would I want to force someone whose heart is not in it to participate in one of the most important days of my life? Should I go to a Mosque and ask a Mullah to perform a wedding in the name of Christ? Should I sue him if he fails to provide the service? It's obvious that doing so is inherently wrong, and yet liberal/progressive judges are ignoring business' rights and siding with the complainants. The truth is that one's rights end where someone else's begins. Why should someone's sexual orientation trump another's faith and beliefs? Religious freedom does not evaporate just because an individual runs a business.

As examples, recently a bakery was sued for refusing to bake a cake for a gay wedding as well as a Bed & Breakfast for not allowing a gay wedding in their home. In both cases the owners were Christians and believed supporting a gay wedding went against their faith. The media ripped the businesses apart, failing to report that the bakery made cakes and other treats for homosexuals for other events. They simply would not make a wedding cake for a gay marriage. The B&B had no problem hosting wedding receptions and housing gay couples, they just did not want the wedding to take place in their house. Both businesses were ruled against and forced to pay fines to the plaintiffs. In both cases the owners have chosen to discontinue their disputed services rather than go against their beliefs. They may have lost income, but not their morals and certainly not their souls.

If we are suppose to be more tolerant, why do we see so little tolerance from those that shout it the loudest? Tolerance means to accept me as I am. I am a Christian. My faith, like that of Jews and Muslims, is that marriage is between a man and a woman. We believe that God instituted marriage, not governments. So why do you attack me for my beliefs? I simply ask that you be more tolerant and accepting of those different from you.

Of course, that's just my 2 cents.

Love,
Mom

Is Justice Blind?

September 24, 2014

Dear Liberty,

On this day 225 years ago, President George Washington signed into law the Judiciary Act of 1789. As outlined in the Constitution, the First Congress was tasked with establishing the federal court system under one Supreme Court. The new court would have a Chief Justice and five Associate Justices. President Washington began appointing these positions immediately.

Many Anti-Federalist Founding Fathers wanted to stop here. They feared a large, strong judiciary would allow the federal government to use the courts to become tyrannical, eradicating state and individual rights. To relieve the critic's concerns, the Bill of Rights was written to establish certain rights that the courts could not take away.

Creating a balance between state and central government powers, the Judiciary Act designed our current federal system to include the Supreme Court at the top, followed by circuit courts and district courts throughout the states. This structure meant a case would have been heard and ruled on several times before it could be heard by the Supreme Court.

Interestingly, this is very much the system used by Moses and the Israelites while they were in the desert during the exodus. After Moses realized he could not hear all the cases that needed to come before him, his father-in-law advised him to find honest, trustworthy, men of truth that he would place as rulers over thousands, hundreds, fifties and tens. Only the cases too difficult to be handled at a lower level were brought before Moses himself.

To protect the people from an overreaching court system, the Bills Of Rights was written specifically to give the states authority over issues not assigned to one of the three federal branches. As you might imagine, this Bill of Rights is viewed by some in the federal government as an obstacle. President Obama described the Constitution as a "charter of negative liberties", lamenting that it puts limits on the federal government's ability to control people's lives.

The Bill of Rights was all about what the government can't do to you, not what they can do to you or for you. It limited the government's ability to redistribute your wealth to others, to take away your choice of food, limit and even abolish your gun ownership, and remove your freedom of speech and religion. As the Anti-Federalist feared, Obama's administration is doing everything it can to use the courts to eradicate our personal freedoms and rights. At this same time it is suing states that are enforcing laws that the federal government is mandated to enforce, such as immigration.

This isn't the first time that the Executive Branch has used the courts for its own interests. The Judiciary Act of 1869 increased the number of justices from 6 to 9, thus allowing President Ulysses S. Grant to appoint one justice immediately. This loading of the bench helped him achieve court rulings in his favor for Reconstruction initiatives.

In similar fashion, President Franklin D. Roosevelt found his New Deal policy hamstrung by the Supreme Court as it ruled it unconstitutional. He tried desperately to "stack the court" by introducing a bill that would allow him to appoint up to 6 more judges. While trying to pass his judicial bill in 1937, which stalled in Congress and eventually died, he continued to apply heavy pressure on the court to reverse their decision on the New Deal. His efforts eventually worked, allowing one of the worst pieces of progressive legislation to date to be ruled Constitutional. His efforts, meant to benefit the common man, instead resulted in a tremendous burden being forced on already struggling citizens, hampering the poor's ability to rise out of poverty. The sales pitch and ultimate result of the New Deal were polar opposites. In that way, it is eerily similar to ObamaCare.

ObamaCare, or the Affordable Care Act (ACA), was forced on the American people and pushed through the Supreme Court by Chief Justice Roberts. The ACA required everyone purchase insurance or pay a mandated fine. Several lawsuits were quickly filed with lower courts once Obama signed it into law. The findings in the lower courts were split on the constitutionality of the mandate. As expected, a lawsuit made its way to the Supreme Court. While arguing their case, the Justice Department first maintained the mandate was only a fine as was written in the law. The very next day they insisted the mandate was in fact a tax. This enabled them to get around the Commerce Clause, which allows for a mandated tax but not a fine. Between Justice Roberts' initial vote and the final procedural vote, he mysteriously changed his mind, much to the dismay of fellow conservative justices arguing constitutionality. To the confusion of many, in his majority opinion he maintained the mandate was unconstitutional as a fine, but constitutional as a tax. By this action he deserted his duty to judge legality and rewrote the law to make it legal. Many believe, as with FDR, the Obama Administration put overwhelming pressure on a Supreme Court Justice to vote not for the Constitution or the people, but *for the Administration.*

Some judicial appointments are more about favors or rewards than politics. Republican President Bush nominated close friend and advisor Harriet Miers in 2005, who many deemed unqualified for the appointment and saw it as a "thank you for your support" gesture. She was even recommended by Democrat Senator Harry Reid, one of the most liberal Senators in Congress. It was a complete slap in the face to conservative (brewing Tea Party) Republicans who let him know immediately. Ms. Miers withdrew her nomination about three weeks later, not due to Democrats who opposed her, but her own party.

Other appointments are purely political. Justice Elena Kagan was part of the Obama Justice Department serving as Solicitor General. She spearheaded the enactment of ObamaCare and even defended the act in federal court. For her efforts, she was awarded a seat as a Supreme Court Justice in 2010. Not only was this a payoff for her work, but it allowed the administration to put the very person that argued the case in lower court to hear it at the Supreme Court. Having argued the case, Justice Kagan should have recused herself from the Supreme Court proceedings. After all, she had a vested interest in the outcome. Unfortunately, she proved to have no integrity and remained on the case. Clearly justice would not be blind.

This type of legislation from the bench has become the norm rather than the exception. More and more judges are deciding to rule not on what the Constitution and law says, but on the color of one's skin, gender, economic status, sexuality, or religion. This is known as social justice, using the courts to favor a chosen minority over someone else demeaned to have more.

Social justice seeks to benefit a select group over another. Rather than treat people equally, it's about equality. It's not about being fair, but fairness. Where justice is blind, social justice is clearly not color blind. It seeks to tear down some, while bringing others up. In essence, it's as God revealed in 2 Timothy 3:4,5 "treacherous, reckless, conceited, lovers of pleasure rather than lovers of God, holding to a form of godliness, although they have denied its power; Avoid such men as these." These judges are seeking to do what they deem to be good, when in essence its roots are in evil. They have put themselves in the place of God and are determined to make things right as they see fit.

This is due in part to the eradication of God and the 10 Commandments in our schools, our colleges, businesses and our courthouses. Without God and his guidelines, sin easily takes over. We see no wrong in stealing, murdering, adultery, or abuse. We are numb to the prospect of taking from one person just to give to another. By *removing God from our lives, the American people begin to see no issues with politicians that are sexually immoral, or lie, cheat, and steal. Is it any wonder that we begin to elect to office and appoint as judges people with these traits?*

We have come to a point where many judges are appointed because they DON'T follow the Constitution or the law. In fact, they write law from their bench. Lawyers are even deciding where to file their lawsuits based on the political leanings of the judges. No, Liberty, justice is not blind. Justice has become racist, bigoted, prejudice, heterophobic, anti-Christian, anti-Jewish, ultra-liberal, and overwhelmingly politically correct.

If America wants to restore the liberties and rights the Founding Fathers gave us and millions of Americans have fought and died to preserve, then she must turn back to God. We must start restoring His commands in our own lives and then electing those to serve who have that same commitment to the Lord. We can change Washington only by changing who we send there. As I stated before, Moses found honest, trustworthy, men of truth to serve the people.

We have the answer. The question is, will America hear it?

That's my 2 cents.

Love,
Mom

Actions Speak Louder Than Words

October 2, 2014

Dear Liberty,

Christ told a story of two sons. The father asked the first son to go work in the vineyard. The son replied, "I will not," but changed his mind and went. The father asked the second son the same request. He replied, "I will," but did not go. Which son did what his father wanted?

At the recent People's Climate Rally in New York, thousands of protesters gathered to proclaim their support for environmental issues and urging the government to control people's actions to defend the environment. As the rally drew to an end, participants left the city streets covered with mounds of flyers, leaflets, signs, Styrofoam cups, plastic bottles, and pop cans. This trash littered the streets and sidewalks and spilled out from trash cans, making New York the "City that Never Sleeps (because some people just won't clean up after themselves.)"

Four years ago another large rally took place in Washington DC. This rally was Glenn Beck's Restoring Honor, one of the 1st major Tea Party rallies, hosting an estimated 500,000 participants. When these protesters went home, they left the Mall cleaner than when they arrived.

Actions speak louder than words.

Environmentalists love to preach to the world of the need to love and cherish the Earth, but whose actions showed that respect in their rally? Conservatives and conservationists understand the gift our Heavenly Father gave us with this world and the responsibility we have to protect it. This is known as stewardship, where you as an individual take on the responsibility of looking out for those things that you have been entrusted with. When you take personal responsibility, the big things, such as the environment, fall into place. There are inherent dangers of handing this morality and responsibility over to the government instead of nourishing it in ourselves. By demanding more of government you also risk handing your freedoms, liberty, and possibly souls over to people who are only out for power and control.

Many of the climate change protesters are thrilled that the government has mandated environmental guidelines such as the mpg *standards on cars. They praise the liberal politicians for demanding electric cars while at the same time forcing coal plants to close. These environmentalists believe electricity is clean energy because you get it from the plug in your wall. They have no idea that the electricity they demand for their cars is generated at power plants primarily from burning coal or some other biofuel. They also completely ignore the enormous amounts of carbon emissions released from the private jets and SUVs all the high-profile celebrities force into the atmosphere as they gallivant from one climate change protest to another.*

Instead of letting the free market work, government has decided to become our moral compass with the blessing and support of many. While cutting our oil supply, claiming the need for alternative fuels, Obama also cut funding initiated by President Bush for the development of hydrogen fuels. After GM was bailed out by the Federal Government at taxpayer expense, it was forced to stop production of their hydrogen car in 2009. GM was well on their way to market with hydrogen cars, while Shell geared up to provide the entire fueling infrastructure needed. The feds told the public that this technology was impossible. Today, five years later, GM and Toyota are together pushing for these cars to go to production by 2015, without the help of the government.

Actions speak louder than words.

When the government's not stopping alternative fuels that can work, such as clean burning coal plants or hydrogen fuels, they are funding companies that can't. In 2009 Obama approved a $535 million loan paid by the taxpayers to Solyndra, a solar company that went bankrupt and closed their doors within a few years. The solar panels that they built were not even sold, but destroyed. Many are still wondering where all that money went. This is what happens when governments decide who will be the winners and losers, rather than allowing the market, and therefore the people, to decide.

Environmentalists don't want the underbrush to be touched or removed from national forests, yet it is because of this dry debris that these woods become tinderboxes waiting to be ignited. Privately owned forestlands, where the trees are cut and replanted, suffer far fewer and much less devastating fires than unmanaged Federal land. Forests are healthier when man provides stewardship, not when they are left alone.

Wind power is the nirvana of power to environmentalists, but leads to the death of thousands of birds each year. Senator Ted Kennedy, a longtime liberal environmentalist politician, loved to promote and brag about alternative energy, but fought and defeated a proposed wind farm that would have been in his back yard. Kennedy's nephew, Robert Kennedy Jr., a lawyer and activist present at the recent

New York rally, was asked by a reporter if he would lead by example and give up his cell phone and car. After becoming visibly irritated with the questioning, he said the quality of life should not be sacrificed for the environment. Except that's exactly what they are asking you to do. What do the environmentalists propose we do, if not radically change modern life? Something they themselves are reluctant to do.

Actions speak louder than words.

Liberty, these are not environmental decisions. These are decisions made by politicians and governments for their own gain, promoting their own agenda while using people with good intentions to demand action. The Communists revolutionaries of the Soviet Empire had a name for such sincere people – 'Useful Idiots'. (see <u>Useful Idiots</u>-Vol.2) Considering all the signs degrading capitalism and supporting socialism, communism and revolution at the New York "climate" rally, my statement is fully validated. The rally was never about the environment, it was about promoting government control.

People on the left and the right actually stand behind the government when their morals are being pushed. But when you give the government that power, what do you do when they demand actions you don't agree with? The majority of people oppose same-sex marriage, but the government is punishing and fining people and businesses if they choose not to agree. Nearly 80% of the US population does not agree with non-conditional abortion, especially in late term pregnancies, but the government is telling us we have to allow all abortions or we are denying women a basic right.

The Affordable Care Act (ACA) passed Congress because it would not provide for abortions and the President confirmed that it would not. The President got the votes needed with that assurance, but within weeks of passing the act, he reneged on his promise and the government began forcing businesses and taxpayers to provide abortions. Sarah Palin was mocked for stating the act provided for 'death panels' for the elderly. Just last month, Dr. Ezekiel Emanuel, the author of the ACA, stated that people don't need to live past 75, confirming what Palin had warned. Emanuel went as far as to say that people over 75 shouldn't take medicines, antibiotics or any life-saving instruments because there is no need to prolong their life. By giving up our individual sovereignty, we allow the government to decide if we should come into this world and when we should leave.

You first, Emanuel. Actions speak louder than words.

Isn't it interesting that the same radicals of the 1960s that said don't trust anyone over 30 are now the same people in positions of power? Using basic deductive logic I'll have to agree with them. Don't trust anyone in power.

Former New York City Mayor Michael Bloomberg actively mandated his citizens and businesses conform to his moral standards. He regulated things like guns, salt, the size of pop, and how much trans fat you can get at a restaurant. Even some extreme liberals, such as Whoopi Goldberg, were pushed to their limit. The problem is New Yorkers stood by for so long letting Bloomberg regulate whatever he wanted that they had no footing to prevent him from taking over something they cared about. Bloomberg, with all his mighty rhetoric about defending the environment, would leave his car running for hours so the air conditioner could run while he was in meetings. Let's face it, you can't be too hot when you're fighting global warming.

Actions speak louder than words.

No matter what the intentions, it is not the government's job to shape our morality. That is God's job. But as I have stated in many of my letters to you, Liberty, the government wants desperately to be your god. "They traded the truth about God for a lie. So they worshiped and served the things God created instead of the Creator himself, who is worthy of eternal praise! Amen." Romans 1:25

In his first letter to the Corinthians, Paul wrote, "You say, 'I am allowed to do anything'--but not everything is good for you. And even though 'I am allowed to do anything,' I must not become a slave to anything." He also told us that we should follow God's commands out of love for Him, not as an obligation for salvation. If someone tells you that you MUST follow a certain tradition to be justified in God's eyes, then you MUST reject it.

Martin Luther says that "in the presence of such men" who demand certain behaviors from us, we should, "for the sake of the liberty of faith do other things which they regard as the greatest of sins." The liberal/progressive agenda that forces environmental demands on people is just such an example. This is their religion with government as their god. They have removed the 10 Commandments and replaced them with political correctness. They worship creation along with abortion and same-sex marriage and demand everyone do the same.

I have no problem with telling people about the benefits of cleaner fuels and healthier choices and allowing the people to make their own decisions. If you have a strong enough argument people will buy in. Of course, that's a free market argument and socialists don't believe in that. So they command, demand, tax and force the people into using certain products while taking away others. However, those that are in positions of power are never under the same expectations.

Actions speak louder than words.

That's my 2 cents.

Love,
Mom

What is Columbus Day?

October 13, 2014

Dear Liberty,

Today we celebrate the 522th anniversary of Columbus discovering the New World. Although Leif Eriksson and his Vikings landed in the Americas 500 years before Columbus did, it was Columbus' travels that brought steady communication and trade between the New World and the Old World and eventually colonization.

Columbus began sailing as a teenager on a merchant ship. In 1470 his ship was attacked and sank. He survived, floating to shore on a piece of wood. Once on land he traveled to Lisbon where he studied navigation, map making, mathematics and astronomy. Carefully analyzing wind patterns, he noticed that they traveled east to west in the northern Africa area, now known as trade winds. Further north, along the coasts of France and Spain, winds traveled west to east, known as westerlies. Believing the circumference of the earth was smaller than generally accepted, Columbus was positive one could sail west directly to Asia driven by the trade winds instead of having to travel completely around the African continent. He could then sail back riding on the westerlies.

A devote Catholic, Columbus was convinced he was chosen by God to discover this new route to Asia. It would allow not only for easier trade, but more importantly, it would allow the spread the Gospel to the eastern World. Queen Isabel of Spain shared Columbus' desire for both trade and mission. While other benefactors rejected his plan, she took a gamble in supporting his dangerous voyage. In return, Columbus would collect gold, pearls, and other fine jewels and riches for Spain.

Columbus and his crew left on their journey on the evening of August 2, 1492, after the fiesta of Our Lady of Angels. It was a day of thanksgiving and prayers, a very special tradition to the sailors and their families. Columbus felt it was extremely important to have this time of worship before setting off on this unprecedented voyage. They sailed for 70 days, spotting land in the Bahamas on October 12th. Thinking he landed in the Indies, he referred to the natives as "Indians", a name which remains even to this day, though many have adopted the term Native Americans.

89

The only island that proved to benefit the explorer in gold production was the island the Spanish called Hispaniola, now known as Haiti and the Dominican Republic. It was inhabited by peaceful natives called Taino, or Arawaks. Taino formed a friendship with Columbus and his crew. Columbus set up a fort and colony on this island populating it with several crewmembers.

Progressives, actively trying to rewrite history, claim that when Columbus arrived the natives of Central and Northern America were all living in harmony. Progressives idealize the native people as all being like the Taino, living in a coveted utopia that the white man destroyed. They believe this so much a Seattle school has decided to celebrate Indigenous Day instead of Columbus Day as a statement of their rejection of Columbus. What progressives fail to reveal is among these peaceful indigenous people were the savage, cannibalistic Caribs who moved from island to island in the Caribbean conquering, slaughtering, and eating every Taino in sight. During a later voyage Columbus even lost crew members to the savage behavior of the Caribs.

Another example of the "peaceful" indigenous people in the area were the Aztecs of Mexico. Though more advanced than most other native cultures, they worshipped the god Huitzilopochtli that required 1000 human sacrifices yearly at each of the 300 temples built for his worship. It has been estimated that 1 out of every 5 children in Mexico was sacrificed to their god. It is also believed no less than 50,000 Mexicans were sacrificed every year. In a special ceremony dedicating the temple in modern day Mexico City, 80,000 Mexicans were sacrificed over a four-day period. Sounds a lot like the practices to the pagan god Moloch in the Old Testament. (See <u>"Soylent Green Is Made Out Of People!"</u>) This is who the progressives what us to celebrate instead of Columbus? Is this what they want our country to be?

It has been recorded in numerous studies the violence and war-like tendencies of Native American tribes all over the North American continent before Europeans ever set foot on land. Yes, there were friendly and nice tribes that Europeans did treat horribly. There were also violent tribes that attacked and slaughtered peaceful whites as they settled in villages. There is blame on both sides, each claiming just righteousness in killing others. History is overflowing with such violence with one nation or tribe attacking another. Knowing this, why should we give up our freedoms and liberty for the mistakes of men 400 years ago?

Columbus is criticized for bringing disease to the Americas and devastating the natives living here. Yes, it was a horrible, dreadful result of the European arrival to the area but it was in no way intentional. Because of that "sin", though, this administration claims we must therefore accept the illegals coming across the southern border with all types of infectious diseases. The CDC just informed us that it is our duty to allow people to enter from West Africa that may be infected with the Ebola virus. Apparently we are racist if we don't.

It's laughable the contradictions in the progressive theology. We are to abhor the Italian Christopher Columbus sent by Spain for the destruction, disease and conflict that he and his fellow Europeans brought to America. However, we are supposed to open our arms freely to the Hispanics coming to America bringing destruction, disease and conflict. We are to hate one and embrace the other without complaint, all in the name of political correctness. Progressives in both parties are so busy trying to present themselves as not being racists that they are willingly put the lives of every American at risk of deadly diseases.

It is true Columbus did have his faults. If Columbus had been perfect, he wouldn't have been human. He planned to sail around the world based on his scientific examination of the winds. He failed, but in doing so he discovered a new land and people unknown to the Western world. He was not a great administrator, which is where his negative image originated. Out of frustration and illness, he made the horrible decision to enslave many natives, sending 500 back to Spain for Queen Isabel. She was outraged, claiming the natives were her "subjects" and that enslavement of citizens was against Spanish law. She released them immediately. This whole incident did force a debate in Spain that concluded with the highest officials in both religious and governmental positions to agree that the natives' souls were not only equal to the white man's soul in the eyes of God, they deserved the same rights as any Spaniard in the eyes of the law. Unfortunately, Europe did not afford this consideration to other nationalities and continued their practice of slavery, which they brought to America. Over the years, Columbus was reprimanded repeatedly for his actions or lack there of, such as failing to control the Spaniards in his command, and was eventually arrested and returned to Spain where Queen Isabel relieved him of his governorship duties.

Despite all that, Columbus' mistakes as a civil leader does not diminish the amazing contributions he made as a sailor and explorer. Because of his efforts he ended cannibalism and human sacrifice in the area and brought Christianity to a world that had never enjoyed the freedoms of faith in Jesus Christ. If he had not discovered America, then America would not have been here to have the ongoing debate and discussion on the morality of slavery, which eventually ended in war. A war that not only ended slavery in the US, but also signaled the death chime of slavery in Europe, where it came from. America would not have been here to fight the Germans and save millions of Jews. America would not be here to send aid and comfort to billions all over the world. I would not be here. You would not be here.

Though there were other instances of abuse and forced labor from the Spanish onto the natives, many worked voluntarily on the farms and in the mines on Hispaniola. Those who wished to remain absolutely and completely free of Spanish rule did so undisturbed in the mountains. Many native women happily married the Spaniards coming to the area and lived willingly in the colonies with their husbands. Their lives did change, but one could argue for the better. Any enslavement that did occur ended after the original settlers were gone.

Progressives are constantly proclaiming that we need to move forward, chart new courses and invariably force their beliefs on those all over the world. In the same way, Columbus set out to chart a new course and move in a new direction in his own time. However, progressives crucify him for forcing the Western world on people who did not want such progress. In a liberal's eyes, Columbus and America must pay for Columbus' sins forever, even as they follow in his same path. They charge him with bringing disease from another nation and accuse he should have known better. Today we are doing exactly the same thing. Our current administration promotes policies of allowing open borders without attempting to prevent the spread of diseases such as Ebola or even terrorists threats. However, unlike Columbus, if a liberal policy has negative consequences they will never be held accountable because their intentions are promoted as good and that's all that matters.

Liberal/Progressive logic dictates that we must condemn Columbus for bringing disease, slavery, and other European issues to the Americas. Apparently, they claim the only way to redeem ourselves is to become exactly like Europe. Wouldn't logic dictate that if progressives were really angry with Columbus, shouldn't they reject the philosophy that brought him here in the first place? And our country did do just that. It was called the Revolutionary War.

Yes, the vast majority of our ancestors came to this country from Europe, bringing their culture and traditions, but they eventually desired separation from the ruling elite. Those coming to American after it won it's independence were largely fleeing from the oppressive, tyrannical, binding governments of the countries the liberal/progressives want us so desperately to return to. They should be celebrating our independence and separation from the imperial Europeans. Instead, they want us to go back to a time of slavery, suppression of women and minorities, and monarchies.

As much as they hate Columbus for finding America, they are desperate to cling to the benefits this country has granted them. But as I have told you before in previous letters, for progressives, it's not about our past and the mistakes America has made. It's not even about repenting and repaying for those sins. It's about power. And how do they get that power? They find a way to make you feel guilty and then use that guilt to control you. Don't fall for the trap, Liberty. Educate yourself. Find the truth, learn the truth, live the truth and spread the truth.

Happy Columbus Day, Liberty. Thank you, God, for giving us America.

That's my 2 cents.

Love,
Mom

Keeping The Faith

October 20, 2014

Dear Liberty,

 Recently the Houston, Texas city council passed an ordinance allowing transgenders to use the public facilities of their choice. However, critics point out male sexual predators can use this to dress as women to enter female facilities to watch and potentially harm or rape girls and women. In efforts to overturn this ordinance, faith-based organizations coordinated petition signature drives to force a public vote on the issue. After the city secretary confirmed there were enough signatures, the city lawyer decided unilaterally that over 2000 were invalid and dismissed the petition. The organizations filed a lawsuit against the city which responded by charging that several pastors participated in the city ordinance protest and subpoenaed their sermons. However, the pastors are not part of the actual lawsuit. The city decided to target these pastors in efforts to intimidate and paralyze the faith-based groups from continuing with their lawsuit.

 Liberals have so turned the First Amendment on it's head that the Houston mayor, Annise Parker, who happens to be gay, believes she not only has the right to ask for and review the sermons, she has the right to threaten the pastors with their tax exempt status. After 60 years of repeating "separation of church and state", people today actually believe it is part of the Constitution. It is not. Much of this deliberate misinformation by liberal politicians stems from the 1947 Supreme Court case of Everson vs. Board of Education, which sited "separation of church and state" in their ruling. They claimed the Founding Fathers built a solid wall between the two entities that must be preserved. Unfortunately the justices invoked a policy that was never part of the Founders' framework but has corrupted American culture ever since. (see <u>Separation Of Church And State</u> – Vol. 2)

 The term "separation of church and state" was originally used by President Thomas Jefferson in 1801 in a private letter addressing a specific question from the Baptist church. The Danbury Baptists were concerned the First Amendment from the Bill of Rights implied religious freedom was granted by the government and not by God, or inalienable. They were worried that one day the government might try to regulate the church's beliefs and traditions. Jefferson's letter makes it clear the government is strictly prohibited from dictating the actions, practices and speech of the church, not the other way around. However, *this is exactly what the Houston mayor is attempting to do. It never meant that churches and pastors could not participate, protest or be activists in the political arena. Ironically liberals are doing exactly what the Baptists were concerned about and what Jefferson said the government was explicitly not allowed to do when he used that phrase. Jefferson was in no way saying there was a wall limiting free religious public expression. He was instead putting the yoke of limitation on the government's right to interfere with that expression.*

When the Founding Fathers wrote the Bill the Rights, they were protecting the people from this very behavior of an overreaching government. The First Amendment was purposefully put first to show that your ability to speak your mind without fear of governmental threat is central to freedom. Americans have the right to say and believe whatever they want. This includes political statements from the pulpit. The Politically Correct police are desperately doing everything they can to guilt and shame you into silence. They have convinced Americans that pastors are prohibited from political comments. That is not freedom and it stomps all over your liberty.

In the early days of America most little towns had a few businesses and a church. That church often served not only as the local place of worship, it was also the school, the town meeting hall, and the location of many social events. Public prayers would accompany these events and any religious symbols would remain proudly displayed for everyone to see. The church was the center of the town. It would have been inconceivable for the Founder's to demand a wall be built between the church and government.

Democrat Senator Lyndon Johnson in 1954 saw an opportunity to start controlling religious rejection of the liberal and progressive agenda by offering the Johnson Amendment. He added religious organizations to the tax-exempt 501c3 status code claiming he was helping churches. As churches started receiving this status, many were threatened with the loss of this privilege if they spoke out against certain politicians, parties, or policies. This is a complete violation of the First Amendment and a far cry for the left's precious separation of the two institutions. Because of the Constitution's guarantee of freedom of religion accompanied with the First Amendment's protection that "Congress shall make no law respecting an establishment of religion, nor prohibiting the free exercise thereof", churches were never taxable because they are not under the control of the government.

Democrats demand separation if they believe a church is in anyway associated with a Republican. The news media harasses the politician until they have to publicly detach from the church and apologize. Democrats, though, freely address black congregations and campaign at churches, some even speaking from the pulpit. President

Obama's minister damned America from the pulpit for its past, he was criticized by the right, but supported for his view by the left. Shouldn't the left have demanded that his tax-exempt status been revoked? Political statements in the church are fine if they agree with gay rights, hatred of America, or environmental issues.

In Houston the mayor is now backtracking. She has suffered a significant backlash from the national awareness of her subpoena. The pastors held to their First Amendment rights and brought awareness to this unconstitutional demand. After tweeting the sermons were "fair game", Parker is now claiming she didn't know the subpoenas even requested them. It is a shameful display of lawlessness and an out of control government. Even though the city is retreating from wanting sermons, they claim it is only because the subpoenas were too broad in their requests. Promises have been made to clarify the information needed by the city. This is not over by a long shot. That's what "progress" is all about. The Progressive movement is just Communism without the revolution. They progress slowly towards total government control.

Liberty, your freedoms, your rights, and your independence are constantly in jeopardy of being taken from you by deceit, manipulation, or outright force. You must constantly be vigilant of the government's actions, both local and national. America became lazy in regards to holding our politicians accountable for the promises they made and broke, the laws they passed, the judges they approved and appointed, and their overall moral and ethical behavior. We can't let that happen any more. If God answers our prayers and your dad and I are able to pass a free America on to you, I pray you and your generation do a better job of being "We the People" than we did. I hope our generation is waking up before it is too late.

That's my 2 cents.

Love,
Mom

Love The One You're With

October 24, 2014

Dear Liberty,

I read an article today about a 69-year old woman in the UK who wishes she had aborted her 47-year old son who suffers from Down Syndrome. Having relatives with this condition, I know it is a difficult situation. What troubles me, though, is her reasoning and callousness.

"We would have had a normal family life." "Stephen...has brought a great deal of stress and heartache into our lives." Before they judge us "they should know how it feels to watch Stephen's constant suffering and witness the almost daily destruction wreaked on all our lives." "I know our lives would have been happier and far less complicated if he had never been born."

I can't deny this woman's pain and suffering. It is real. But Liberty, I want to remind you that in situations like this, we must turn to God for guidance and strength. We are not promised perfect lives. We are not promised perfect children. But as a child of God it is our response and our attitude towards these trying times that not only strengthens our own faith, but are examples of Christ's love for others.

This woman laments every day that she did not have an abortion. How sad to live your life that way. She's sorry her son has the life he has but she tends to quickly turn to how it disrupted her plans. She's miserable and she blames her son. I would like to point out that she lead the life she chose. Not one with a special needs child but one drenched with hurt, regret, disappointment, and despair. She believes her life would have been happier with another child, but who's to say that child wouldn't have some other issue, or become a drug addict, or severely injured in an accident leaving them in constant need of care?

When I was pregnant with you, Liberty, there was a moment where a test result revealed a heightened possibility of you having Down Syndrome. Your father and I were scared and I won't lie, it made me wonder what kind of life you would have. I wondered how caring for a special needs child would change our lives in ways far more different than having a "normal" child. But there was never a second, not even a thought, of terminating the pregnancy. We knew God would not give us more than we could handle and I was going to love you for who you were.

One of my co-workers at the time found out about the test results and came to tell me about his Down Syndrome child. He told me of how loving and kind his son was, more so than any of his other children. It was comforting. I spent time talking to other co-workers as well trying to work through the possibilities before me. One of them told me after you were born that she was impressed by how I handled the news and how my display of faith inspired her. I'm telling you this, Liberty, not to brag but as an example of how we, as God's children, affect others by everything we do. The day we got the test results was one of the worst days of my life. Yet by clinging desperately to my Heavenly Father, instead of cursing Him as our sinful nature wants to do, He used me as a witness to someone else even in a very trying time for me.

We were blessed to find out that you did not have Down Syndrome. We rejoiced and praised God for His blessing. I feel for this woman, though. Not because of her son's condition, but because she was unable to see his beauty and uniqueness beyond that condition. I'm heartbroken that she was unable to embrace her circumstance and make the best of it instead of living a life of sorrow for 47 years. She said she loves her son, but how can you love someone you wished was dead every day of his life? What's even worse is I'm sure her son knows how she feels. And that's the most tragic part of all.

That's my 2 cents.

Love,
Mom

The Knock Heard 'Round The World

October 31, 2014

Dear Liberty,

BANG! BANG! BANG! The knock at the door sent reverberations through the night sky and deep into the foundation of the church. The first nail was driven into the coffin of the Catholic Church. The parchment hung for all to see. It was a simple note but it would turn out to be the Pope's worst nightmare.

The story begins in 1483. The printing press was invented 30 years before (see *All In Due Time* – Vol. 2), the Spanish Inquisition was 3 years old (see *The American Inquisition* – Vol. 2), and a decade before Columbus braved the uncharted seas (see *What Is Columbus Day?*). The birth of Martin Luther was not an extraordinary one, but it was one that would impact the world forever.

A devote Catholic, Luther never even read the Bible until a Latin class in college. In those days Bibles were exclusively in Latin. Only priests, monks and some universities had access to them. Due largely to the fact that each Bible was handwritten, it took years to produce a single copy. Well on his way to becoming a lawyer, Luther was not seeking any position in the church other than a seat in a pew during Mass.

That all changed during a thunderstorm. A bolt of lightening struck dangerously close to Luther, overwhelming him with fear. He vowed to devote himself to God if his life was spared. His prayer was answered. Even though it was tearing him apart to leave law school, within a matter of weeks he had left the University of Erfurt for the monastery to fulfill the promise he made.

Luther was not an enthusiastic monk at first but he was determined to move forward with this new chapter in his life. While at the monastery Luther was able, for the first time, to really study the Bible. Luther spent hours fasting and praying trying to feel forgiven of his sins. He would even sleep naked on the floor, basically torturing himself, trying to earn salvation. Nothing Luther did, no good work, would bring him the comfort and freedom he was searching for. Nothing he did seemed to be good enough.

With prodding from his vicar, Luther extended his studies to *become a priest as well as a Doctor of Theology. After years of study and despair in his ability to do enough works to justify his salvation, Luther found the answer he was craving. "For in the gospel the righteousness of God is revealed--a righteousness that is by faith from first to last, just as it is written: 'The righteous will live by faith.'" (Romans 1:17) It was this verse that revealed the true grace of God our Father and the gift of our Lord and Savior Jesus Christ. It is by faith alone that saves us. Faith in Christ, his death on the cross and his resurrection freed us from the chains and punishment of sin.*

This revelation sent Luther back through the rest of the scriptures, focusing on the Psalms and Paul's writings, for more explanation and clarification. He realized his Catholic faith was a religion of works based salvation. Wanting to open discussion and debate regarding his new revelation, Luther found his opportunity when a monk in Saxony decided to peddle his indulgences. The Catholic Church had decided that the people could purchase God's appeasement, buying their way out of temporal punishment for their sins by prayer, good works, but mostly by money. Luther realized forgiveness of sins is set purely and completely on the shoulders of Christ. It has all been forgiven through grace. Indulgences were just a form of tax the church put on the people to raise money. One could compare it to the moneychangers in the temple that infuriated Christ causing him to overturn tables. The leadership in the Catholic Church had become a den of thieves.

Feeling that indulgences were evil, Luther took the occasion to write 95 theses, or arguments, against indulgences, good works, the papacy, and other relevant theological issues. He posted his theses on October 31, 1517, on the town bulletin board, which was the All Saints' Church door in Wittenberg where he was a professor at the University.

Initially Luther's statement did not gather much attention. It wasn't until three months later, when some of Luther's friends translated the 95 theses into German from the original Latin, did word begin to spread. Using the relatively new invention the printing press, copies were printed and circulated throughout Germany within two weeks, in two months throughout all of Europe. It was one of the very first times the printing press was used to forward a movement. A fire was ignited that could not be extinguished. Only wanting to open debate, Luther found himself in the middle of a war that seemed one uphill battle after another. An inquisition was brought upon him, which could mean his life. Refusing to recant his statements and writings, Luther was eventually excommunicated from the Catholic Church. Fearing for his life he was forced to go into hiding for a year in Wartburg Castle. His confinement proved to be a blessing. It was here that Luther translated the Bible into German. With help of the printing press, millions of commoners were given the ability to read the Bible for the first time in history.

Luther came to realize that Christ destroyed the wall that stood between God and his people. As our mediator Christ allowed people to have direct, personal access to God. Over several centuries the Catholic Church rebuilt and expanded the wall that separated the people from God. Congregants were required to pray to Mother Mary along with appointed Saints for every issue at hand. Luther realized this was a complete denial of Christ's purpose. If one could access God through someone other than Christ, or if they could earn their own salvation, than what was the purpose of Christ's death? Luther broke down this false wall, revealing Christ as our personal access to God. He wrote a new mass and hymns. Utilizing everything to teach God's Word, Luther used direct Biblical verses to write hymn lyrics as well as prayers and chants during the service.

Though Luther was in no way the only leader in the Protestant Reformation, he was the most well known. He tried to compromise, hoping to build a unified faith. Following a disagreement with Ulrich Zwingli of Switzerland on the sacraments, Luther could no longer deny his understanding of God's Word. He did find agreement with many others and together they composed the Book of Concord, which is the foundation of the Lutheran doctrine. He also wrote the Large Catechism, an in-depth explanation of God's Word, along with the condensed Small Catechism, which was designed for parents to use to teach their children.

Liberty, we celebrate Reformation because it is the movement that gave rebirth to the Gospel of Jesus Christ. It opened our eyes to the truth of justification by faith alone. Up until this point those in the Roman Catholic Church were forced to believe whatever the priests told them as they had no access to the bible themselves. Because of Luther's German translation and the ability to mass print Bibles, we are able to read, mark, learn and inwardly digest God's Word directly. This is partially why the copies of his 95 theses were so quickly absorbed throughout the area. Many felt the burdens and guilt imposed by a works based faith. The peace they received from a salvation from grace by faith allowed them the freedom to love their God without shame and without fear, worshiping Him out of pure and honest thanksgiving.

I am not condemning Catholics, I am describing the faults of the church leadership and Luther's attempts to correct it. Just as I can do that, though, Catholics can find many statements from Luther that could convict him as well. To which I would say "He is human. Of course he had faults." Luther himself was well aware of his sinfulness and inadequacies. He never wanted to start a new faith and definitely did not want that new church to be called Lutheran. He believed anyone following Christ's teachings should be called simply Christian. As he so eloquently stated, "The first thing I ask is that people should not make use of my name, and should not call themselves Lutherans but Christians. What is Luther? The teaching is not mine. Nor was I crucified for anyone...How did I, poor stinking bag of maggots that I am, come to the point where people call the children of Christ by my evil name?" Which is why, Liberty, you cannot blindly follow anyone other than Christ. We are Lutheran's because we believe he correctly taught the true meaning of the Bible. We in no way worship him or put his writings over the Bible. We compare for consistency and if there is a discrepancy than the authority of the Bible should always win out.

Luther's goal was to return the Catholic Church to the Theology of the Cross. Once removed from the church, he chartered a new course to preach the true Gospel of Jesus Christ. (see <u>Here I Stand</u>-Vol.4) Despite his objections, a denomination did emerge using his name only to distinguish itself from the other Protestant churches beginning to develop. Under the Roman Catholic Church, the task of interpreting the Bible fell squarely on the shoulders of the Pope. It was not uncommon then for the church to change its beliefs when a new Pope was appointed. As people started breaking from the Catholic Church, the freedom to interpret the Bible was embraced by others and not left to only one man. People could then follow which understanding they believed to be correct.

So as you dress up on this day in cute little outfits, knocking on doors for candy, remember the knock that revolutionized faith for Christians over 500 years ago. For believers this day is not just about costumes and candy, it is also a day of liberation. It gave freedom to the world to not only have a choice but an active role in their faith. It is because of Luther we have direct access to God's Word. It proves that one man can make a difference. One man can change the world.

That's my 2 cents.

Love,
Mom

November 3, 2014

Dear Liberty,

Tomorrow is election day. After months of confusing, deceptive and outright misleading political ads, I would like to dispel some falsehoods that have saturated the progressive political agenda over the past 50 years. I hope to expand on some of the claims in later letters to you, but here is a quick look at several charges made against the Republican Party and the truth regarding the issue.

Charge - The Republican Party is racist.
Fact - The Republican party began in the 1850's by a group of abolitionists, including both Whigs and Democrats, who were tired of their respective parties claiming they were going to solve the slavery issue but never acted. Their main goal was to end slavery. It is important to note that during the Civil War the anti-slavery North elected a Republican as President while the pro-slavery South elected a Democrat, Jefferson Davis. (see The Birth Of A Movement*)*

Charge - The Republican Party still wants slavery.
Fact - President Lincoln, the first Republican President, gave his life to free slaves. He was assassinated by John Wilkes Booth, a Southern Democrat, who was furious that Lincoln ended the South's way of life. Lincoln knew his life was on the line because of his actions on slavery. However, knowing it was the right thing to do, he stood firm in proclaiming freedom for all.

Charge - Republicans don't see African-Americans as whole people.
Fact - The Constitutional Convention of 1787 designed the census procedures, which would determine the number of House members for each state. Southern Delegates wanted slaves to be counted even though those men and women were considered property and weren't allowed to vote for elected officials. Northern delegates recognized this strategy by the slave owners to pack the House with Southern representatives. This would ensure the leadership, legislation, and votes in the House would be almost completely controlled by the South. It was essentially taxation without representation. Slaves were going to be used to increase representation in the House, but that representation would be for slave owners almost guaranteeing ongoing enslavement. Trying to avoid this possibility, Northern delegates

resisted counting the slaves. The Southern delegates would hear nothing of it. A compromise was reached counting slaves as 3/5ths of a person. Not because the North didn't believe they were fully human, but in attempts to give abolitionists a fighting chance to end slavery through a political process. After the Civil War, it was the recently formed Republican Party that pushed through the 13th Amendment that abolished slavery. This eliminated the 3/5ths rule and counted the newly freed slaves as equals to the whites.

Charge - The Republicans have always kept minorities down.
Fact - Lincoln, the 1st Republican President, not only signed the Emancipation Proclamation, which freed Confederate slaves, he put in motion law after law giving freedoms and liberties to recently freed slaves. After his assassination, Vice President Andrew Johnson, a Southern Democrat, immediately started revoking all of Lincoln's advancements for the black population. While Republicans fought for control of the Reconstruction era and rights for the newly freed slaves, Johnson argued their future should be left in the hands of the Southern slave owners. Fortunately the Republicans won and the 13th, 14th and 15th Amendments were passed ensuring inalienable rights and liberties to all blacks.

Charge - The Republicans would still have lynchings if they could.
Fact - Lynchings were performed on a routine basis by members of the Klu Klux Klan. The KKK was started and populated by Southern Democrats who were furious that Republican President Lincoln made the black man the same as the white. In fact, lynchings were not just for blacks. 25% of those lynched in the South were white conservatives who supported black rights. As recent as 2010, a former KKK leader was a predominate Senate Democrat. Congressman Robert Byrd claimed he left the KKK to pursue politics, but his true feelings were revealed on multiple occasions. Several times he was recorded using the word nigger on the chamber floor. Not one Democrat (including Al Sharpton and Jesse Jackson) flinched or criticized him or dared to ask him to apologize. Furthermore no Democrat minded that at the time of his death he was longest serving congressman in history. In fact they celebrated it. (see <u>How The South Was Won</u> – Vol. 2)

Charge - Republicans would return to segregation if they could.
Fact - After the Civil War Republicans made amazing strides in desegregating America during the Reconstruction years. When Progressive Democrat Woodrow Wilson entered office he turned back the hands of time a half-century by separating blacks in federal departments, including the military. He went so far as to keep any blacks in the forces in non-combat roles out of fear of teaching them how to handle a gun. He was afraid they might actually gain the ability to defend themselves against racial attacks once the war was over. Wilson claimed it was all for the good and prosperity of the negro. He

removed blacks from federal posts replacing them with whites and allowed the IRS official in Georgia to fire all black employees, claiming the negros' place was in the corn field, not the government. Segregation was started and supported by liberal/progressive Democrats, not Republicans. (see <u>Birth Of A Nation</u> – Vol. 2)

Charge - Republicans are Nazis.
Fact - The Nazi Party represents the National SOCIALIST Party of Germany. Hitler, the leader of the Nazi Party, believed not only in government control, but killed 6 million Jews out of hatred. He started his reign by removing God and guns from his citizen's lives. This is the complete opposite of the supposed "Nazi-like" small government Tea Party. (see <u>Sanger And Eugenics And Socialism, Oh My</u> – Vol. 2)

Charge - Republicans want to put minorities in camps and restricted areas like Hitler did.
Fact - Andrew Jackson, the first Democrat president, pushed through the Indian Removal Act of 1830 authorizing the government to essentially propose deals that eliminated the Indians' rights to the lands in the southeast. The result was the brutal and deadly removal of the Cherokee tribes of the east to west of the Mississippi, otherwise known as the Trail of Tears. It was because of this Act that Native Americans still live on reservations today and as a result, in poverty. (see <u>Satan's Manifest Destiny</u>-Vol.3 and <u>Doctrinally Sound</u>-Vol.4) A little over a century later another beloved Democrat President and progressive champion, Franklin D. Roosevelt, ordered the round up of over 100,000 Japanese and Japanese-Americans. He placed them in concentration camps for the duration of WWII with no evidence of spying or conspiracy every happening. Roosevelt defended his actions due to national security after the bombing of Pearl Harbor. His executive order also affected German-Americans and Italian-Americans. (see <u>Forgotten Atrocities Of WWII</u>-Vol.4) Perhaps if we had been blessed with a Democrat president following September 11th, those with Arabic backgrounds could have been round up. However, with a Republican, that never happened and the people never demanded it.

Charge - The NRA wants to kill blacks.
Fact - When the KKK began their tormenting and murdering campaign, they were often met with resistance by free blacks who armed themselves for personal protection. The Democratic Party in the south, who was often one in the same with the KKK, passed laws denying gun rights to former slaves. This allowed the KKK to perform their "duties" without threat of a serious fight. They even victimized white Republicans that supported black rights. The NRA took action to make sure those being targeted, regardless of race, had the rights to defend themselves. The NRA is accredited with playing a significant role in the civil rights movement, fighting for the rights of all.

Charge - The Republican Party just wants all blacks dead.

Fact - Planned Parenthood, a major proponent of abortions, was founded by activist and feminist Margaret Sanger. Supporters tout her as a predominant voice for birth control. The truth is her goal was not for a woman's choice, but "to create a race of thoroughbreds." A huge champion of eugenics, she believed that if society could eliminate the undesirables, such as blacks and immigrants, then the perfect race would emerge. To gain support for her efforts she often spoke at KKK meetings. "We do not want word to go out that we want to exterminate the Negro population," she said, "if it ever occurs to any of their more rebellious members." According to a recent study, "79% of all Planned Parenthood abortion facilities are located within walking distance of black or Hispanic neighborhoods, or both". Conservative Republican/Tea Party members are fighting to expose the evils and despicable ramifications of this practice. Democrats continue to promote that women should be proud if they wish to kill their baby and ObamaCare pays for them to do it. (see The Axis Of Evil – Vol. 2)

Charge - The Republican Party hates women.

Fact - Condoleezza Rice is an amazing, historical woman. She was the first black woman appointed in two separate top government positions, U.S. National Security Advisor and U.S. Secretary of State. She earned a Ph.D., is a concert pianist and speaks five languages. She should be hailed as the poster woman of the Feminist movement, except she is also a Republican. So instead of the liberal media covering her as an accomplished Black woman, political cartoons used every racial stereotype they could come up with to degrade her while she was in office. When Democrat President Bill Clinton was charged with sexual harassment and rape, the Democrats rallied around him claiming the women were whores, gold diggers, and liars. They destroyed Linda Tripp, who brought the Monica Lewinsky ordeal to light, all while praising Clinton for being able to get a little on the side. The "fairness to women" Democratic Party still continues to rip Sarah Palin apart yet if any Republican says anything about a female liberal they are charged and convicted of sexism. Former Obama Administration Green Czar Van Jones recently admitted to the left's hysteria about Sarah, confessing she had them "shaking in their boots" but now that they have destroyed her, "the truth can be told." The facts clearly show that it is the Democrats who wage a War on Women. (see War On Women – Vol. 2)

Charge - Republicans are all about big business.

Fact - Some of the most influential businesses are run by Democrats. Apple, Microsoft, the film industry, General Motors, Costco, Goldman Sachs, Comcast and AARP to name a few. They have flooded the Democratic coffers with donations to make sure policies are passed to help keep them in the monopoly while destroying mom & pop businesses. Small government Republicans obviously wouldn't be supported by big businesses that need a big government to prevent competition.

Charge - All Republicans want to do is just go to war.
Fact - During the first 75 years of the 20th century, all of the major wars and conflicts America participated in were entered by Democrat presidents. After campaigning never to go to war, Woodrow Wilson committed America to WWI a month after being inaugurated. Franklin D. Roosevelt entered WWII. Due to the Pearl Harbor attack one could argue he had no choice. Harry S. Truman committed our soldiers to Korea and John F. Kennedy sent our boys to Vietnam. It is true that Republicans did lead many of the conflicts with Islamic terrorists during the last quarter of the century but they are hardly the lone instigators in military use.

If politicians and activists are lying about such important issues as these, what else are they lying about?

Now, all this being said, Liberty, I believe the Republican Party has gravely lost its way and has abandoned its roots and principles over the last 25 years. It is the very reason for the birth of the Tea Party conservative movement. You must remember that as much as I can argue the problems in our political parties, we were never meant to put our faith and trust in them anyway.

God is our King. God is our commander. But more importantly, God is our Father. His Word should be our guide and our moral compass. Do we need government? Unfortunately it is a "necessary evil", but when it falls away from God's loving direction for us, we must listen to our Father. Do we purposely defy the government? There are times, though few and far between, that we may have to do that, but we are also told that we must respect government as God has put our leaders in control. We must pray for their safety and for wisdom even if we completely disagree with them. We must also do our best to educate and inform ourselves and then our fellow citizens on the truth and become good and moral individuals. If we do that we will demand moral, honest men and women to serve in our government offices, including local, state and national. That is how real change starts with knowing the truth and changing ourselves.

That's my 2 cents.

Love,
Mom

Happy Veterans Day

November 11, 2014

Dear Liberty,

On the 11th hour of the 11th day of the 11th month of 1918, the fighting in "The Great War" was officially over. Germany, the last of the Central Powers to yield, reluctantly signed a ceasefire agreement with the Allied forces marking the end of World War I. Known as the Armistice of Compiègne, it halted the hostilities until an actual peace agreement could be settled upon and signed 6 months later. The armistice allowed the fighting to cease without Germany having to actually surrender, though it was still considered a defeat of the Central Powers (Germany, Austria-Hungary, Ottoman Empire, Bulgaria) by the Allies (America, Britain, France, Japan, the Russian Empire (until the Revolution), Italy). Although the Central Powers were fighting together, each country signed their own armistices. Final peace with Germany was reached on June 28, 1919, with the signing of the Treaty of Versailles. It was fitting this date was chosen as it marked the 5-year anniversary of the assassination of Austrian Archduke Franz Ferdinand, the event that actually sparked "war to end all wars."

In 1919, President Woodrow Wilson, along with most other Allied leaders, proclaimed November 11th as the holiday 'Armistice Day'. Upon the announcement Wilson said, "To us in America, the reflections of Armistice Day will be filled with solemn pride in the heroism of those who died in the country's service and with gratitude for the victory, both because of the thing from which it has freed us and because of the opportunity it has given America to show her sympathy with peace and justice in the councils of the nations."

Though the day was observed across the nation, it was not made a legal holiday until May 13, 1938, by a Congressional Act declaring it "a day to be dedicated to the cause of world peace and to be thereafter celebrated and known as 'Armistice Day'." Ironically, just two days before the year's Armistice Day celebration, German Jews suffered the Nazi riot known as the Crystal Night (or Kristallnacht). It was the response to a Polish Jew assassinating a German diplomat. Jewish businesses, hospitals, homes, schools, cemeteries and synagogues were vandalized, damaged and destroyed in retaliation. It was dubbed Crystal Night referring to all the broken glass in the streets after the 2-day rampage. German authorities soon required Jews wear a yellow star of David. Fearing for their safety, German Jews also began paying large indemnities. The following year Hitler invaded Poland and within three years the United States entered World War II. The Allies and Central Powers were divided again with the exception of Japan, who changed sides. This war also brought the torture and execution of 6 millions Jews at the hands of the Nazis. World peace was yet to be found.

Armistice Day is still celebrated throughout the world in most Allied nations on or around November 11th. Several counties changed the name after World War II, such as Remembrance Day. In 1954 Congress passed a bill renaming the day 'All Veterans Day', later shortened to 'Veterans Day', so Americans could honor veterans of all wars.

Veterans Day has been observed and celebrated in America on November 11th ever since except for a brief time in the 1970's. Following the Uniform Monday Holiday Act, the holiday was moved to the 4th Monday in October in 1971. It was quickly decided the significance of the date was too important so President Ford returned it to November 11th starting in 1978.

Across the globe, millions stop for a 2-minute moment of silence at 11:00am, honoring the time the last armistice of WWI took effect. Originally the first minute was to reflect on the 20 million lives lost in the conflict while the second minute remembered the loved ones left behind. Many still continue this tradition extending their thoughts to all veterans.

Though we set aside this day to officially recognize and honor the brave men and women who put their lives on the line for freedom and liberty, we should praise these veterans every day. Even if it is just a simple thank you and a handshake, we need to remember and appreciate these men and women who selflessly served their country.

God Bless Our Veterans and God Bless America.

That's my 2 cents.

Love,
Mom

A Tale Of Two Women

November 19, 2014

Dear Liberty,

    This is the story of two women. They both faced the same fate after being diagnosed with terminal brain cancer. They were brave, amazing women that spoke about their struggles, but for very different reasons.

    The first woman was newly married. She learned of her illness on New Year's Day. After an unsuccessful surgery, she was given a six-month window. Anxious about the pain and suffering she was facing, she and her husband moved to Oregon, a "Death with Dignity" state, after deciding to take her own life. Wanting to bring attention to this cause, she partnered with Compassion & Choices to raise awareness for people in her situation.

    In October, she made and posted a video describing her circumstances and announcing her plan to take her own life on November 1st, which was just after her husband's birthday. If she was going to die, she wanted it to be on her terms, at her time, and surrounded by loved ones. The video brought national attention to her cause and the debate over assisted suicide began. Living up to her promise, on the afternoon of November 2nd news broke that she did, in fact, take her own life.

    Several hundred miles away, another young woman was also given a death sentence a year ago. At the time the first woman was diagnosed, the second woman was already coping with the identical prognosis. Not able to find answers as to why this was happening, she decided it didn't matter anyway. She concluded this was God's plan for her. While many that suffer from brain cancer lose the ability to speak, she had not lost hers. She began to act as an advocate for the little children suffering from the same disease who had lost their voice. Her efforts brought attention to the leading cause of death in children. Rather than focus on her circumstances, as the first woman did, she chose instead to fight for others.

    The 19-year-old freshman at Mount St. Joseph played basketball for her school. 5 am practice with the team was debilitating for her, but she didn't want to let her teammates down. She had lost the use of her right arm, so she had to learn to dribble and shoot with the left hand.

But rather than focus on herself and her condition, she practiced and hoped to live long enough to play the opening game. Realizing she was living on borrowed time, the local colleges agreed to move the college woman's basketball season up so she could play in her opening game.

She started the game by making the first basket, but lacked the energy to play anymore until making the team's final shot. Since then she has been speaking out about her cancer, raising awareness and money for the fight. She refuses to give up and believes God is using her. As she expressed many times, her goal is to bring an end to the disease, knowing full well she will not benefit from her efforts. Following the game, she gave a check for $176,000 to Children's Medical Center to search for a cure and gave hope to others facing the same prognosis. By playing the game and partnering with The Cure Starts Now Foundation she brought national attention to her cause. The date was November 2nd, the same day the first woman took her own life.

We make choices every day. Sometimes we have to choose what will be good for us or what will be good for others. It's a tough choice. We all have a desire to put ourselves and our best interests first. And in some cases, we do need to do what's best for us. But regardless of which route your take, Liberty, you must keep in mind that all circumstances can be used to profess God's compassion. How? By how you respond to the roadblocks put in your path. The quality of your character is not built in the good times, but is forged by how you deal with the struggles placed in your life. Are you going to curse and be bitter or are you going to find peace in the saving grace of Our Lord and Savior Jesus Christ. Are you going to try to control things or are you going to let your Heavenly Father guide your life, and in this case, death. Even if the second girl stayed quietly at home, surrounded by family and loved ones in her final days, she would have chosen to leave those days in God's hands. It's also still possible to touch others even if you decide to remain private.

Liberty, this was the case with two of your great-grandmothers. One died of pancreatic cancer, said to be the most painful forms of cancer. In the end there was no amount of morphine that could dull the excruciating pain. Yes, I prayed that God would take her quickly to end her pain and suffering, but I put it in His hands alone, as your great-grandma did. Another of your great-grandmothers died of another form of cancer. She spent the last few weeks of her life in a Hospice facility. While there, where the nurses and attendants see nothing but pain, suffering and agony, your great-grandmother was happy, thankful, and called the workers her angels. While having some tea one day it spilled out of the cup and onto the saucer. Quoting from a poem, she lifted the plate to her lips and said, "I'm drinking from my saucer 'cause my cup has overflowed," referencing Psalm 23. Many of the workers told your grandparents how her attitude and faith were an inspiration to them. They deal daily with people in the last days of their lives. She proved to be a bright star of hope in an otherwise grim circumstance. We can be that ray of hope to others simply by the way we choose to live our lives or experience our death.

I can't image what the two women, 29-year-old Brittany Maynard and 19-year-old Lauren Hill, went through. Brittany fought for herself and ultimately individual rights. Lauren denied herself and fought for others. By facing death, both taught us to live to be something more than we are. What becomes clear is that Brittany's focus on herself left her without hope. Lauren's focus on others gave her purpose. Liberty, live your life focused on others. By doing so, you walk in the very footsteps of Christ and become a witness to His love.

Many will ask how you can worship a God that allows disease, suffering, and death to plague the human race. But how much more glorifying is it to praise a God in those situations than in one of health, happiness, and prosperity? I have had several struggles in my life and I have worn God's ear out praying for answers. I constantly turn to Him, talking to Him and come closer to Him when my life seems otherwise completely out of my control. In those times of smooth sailing, I find myself occupied with other activities, not focusing on my Heavenly Father and talking to Him as I should. It's easy to love and follow God when everything is great. True faith, true reverence, and true trust reveals itself in times of trouble even if the only people to see it are you and God. Fortunately, if that faith is honestly there, it can't help but be exhibited in your daily life.

Liberty, I do pray that you do have a long, healthy, happy life. But when those moments come that are trying, and they will come, it is then that God is giving you an opportunity to truly feel His love for you. Just as you run to your earthly father when you scrape your knee, bump your head or just need to feel his comforting arms around you, I pray you remember you have an Heavenly Father who loves you even more and will console your heart, your mind, and your soul.

That's my 2 cents.

Love,
Mom

Thanks Be To God!

November 27, 2014

Dear Liberty,

A hundred years after Martin Luther nailed his 95 Thesis on the All Saint's Church door, people all over Europe were fighting to worship God as they chose. (see <u>The Knock Heard 'Round The World</u>) Luther and other reformers translated the Bible into multiple languages, giving the people direct access to the Word of God. Thanks to the printing press, designed by Johann Gutenburg in the mid-1400's, thousands of Bibles were printed allowing commoners to read God's Word for themselves for the first time. (see <u>All In Due Time</u> – Vol. 2)

As the freedom of reading the Bible swept through Europe, so did the desire to freely worship God. (see <u>Here I Stand</u>-Vol.4) The people realized they did not need the King or the Pope to tell them what God said, or in some cases, didn't say. Rulers throughout the area, both secular and religious, used a heavy hand to try to squash the new religious sects taking root since the Reformation.

A particular denomination called Separatists, for their desire to separate from the Church of England, fled from England to Holland in 1608 to escape King James' persecution. After taking refuge there for eleven years several members decided to travel to the New World in search of true religious freedom. Since Christopher Columbus' discovery over 120 years earlier, several European rulers had sent explores, workers and settlers to the New World with England overseeing most of the east coast. In this new land there was still oversight from the throne, but there was also freedom and liberty to worship as they chose.

One of the instrumental Separatists, William Bradford, not only organized bringing the Pilgrims to America, he documented their travels and experiences in <u>Of Plymouth Plantation</u>, which is central to knowing the truth of their history. Being orphaned at a young age, he was only 18 when he fled with the Separatists to Amsterdam, then to Leiden. Five years later he married Dorothy May, who was only 16, in 1613. When the couple set off for the Americas in 1620, they left their young son, John, in Holland with relatives, hoping to retrieve him when they got settled in the New World. The one thing Bradford did take along with him was his 1592 Geneva Bible, which would be a *cornerstone of everything he built.*

The Separatists sought and were granted permission via the First Pierce Patent to sail to the Americas and begin the first settlement in the northern part of Virginia Colony. The Separatists hired their friend Captain Myles Standish, a member of Queen Elizabeth's army, to accompany them on their adventure and be their military leader. His expertise was desired to establish and organize the settlement's defense of both foreign (Spanish, Dutch, French) and domestic (Native) foes.

The trip to the New World would take money and the 50 Separatists, or "Saints" as they called themselves, didn't have much of it. They had no choice but to partner with non-Separatists, or "Strangers", to make the trip. Several tradesmen, adventures and servants who were seeking their own opportunities signed on to the voyage.

Beginning in July of 1620, the "Saints" and "Strangers" started their pilgrimage down the English Channel. There were originally two ships, but due to costly repairs for the leaking Speedwell, the passengers all crammed onto the Mayflower before it left its final port in Plymouth, England on September 6/16, 1620. (Two numbers are often given at this time period to show the Julian Calendar date (former) and today's Gregorian Calendar (latter).) (see <u>As Time Goes By</u>-Vol.2) Including the Pilgrims and a 30+ crew led by Captain Christopher Jones, there were 102 passengers in all.

It took two months to reach the New World and it was anything but smooth sailing. Many passengers suffered from seasickness for most of the trip. After a major beam broke, it was feared the ship would have to turn around and go home. Thanks to the supplies brought by the Pilgrims, the beam was reinforced and the trip continued. One passenger, John Howland, fell overboard but miraculously grabbed a topsail halyard that was trailing behind the ship. Passengers were able to pull him back on board unharmed.

On November 9/19, 1620, land was sighted by the crew, but bad weather forced them up the coast from their intended destination in the Virginia Colony to what is now Cape Cod. Since they landed north of their patent's boundaries rendering it invalid, some of the passengers decided this would be an opportunity to challenge the authority granted to the Pilgrim leaders by the patent. Realizing there must be some form of law and order and wanting to encouraged unity and preservation of the group, most colonists agreed to work together to establish a fair government, or civil body politic, promoting justice, equality, and responsibility requiring the consent of the governed. Using the Old and New Testament as their guide, they established the Mayflower Compact that was signed aboard ship on November 11/21, 1620, by most adult men. The Compact was America's first call for freedom. It demonstrates our Christian tradition and values and was a precursor to the Constitution.

Text of Mayflower Compact:

In the name of God, Amen. We whose names are underwritten, the loyal subjects of our dread sovereign Lord, King James, by the grace of God, of Great Britain, France, and Ireland King, Defender of the Faith, etc.

Having undertaken, for the glory of God, and advancement of the Christian faith, and honor of our King and Country, a voyage to plant the first colony in the northern parts of Virginia, do by these presents solemnly and mutually, in the presence of God, and one of another, covenant and combine our selves together into a civil body politic, for our better ordering and preservation and furtherance of the ends aforesaid; and by virtue hereof to enact, constitute, and frame such just and equal laws, ordinances, acts, constitutions and offices, from time to time, as shall be thought most meet and convenient for the general good of the Colony, unto which we promise all due submission and obedience. In witness whereof we have hereunder subscribed our names at Cape Cod, the eleventh of November [New Style, November 21], in the year of the reign of our sovereign lord, King James, of England, France, and Ireland, the eighteenth, and of Scotland the fifty-fourth.

By "accident", or God's hand, these brave men and women were given an opportunity to set up a republic form of government, different than any government seen before. The English settlers before them were part of the English crown where the Pilgrims were considered the true first Americans (not withstanding the Native Americans).

After signing the agreement, the Pilgrims voted John Carver to be the first elected governor in the English colonies. Landing on a Saturday, the group stayed aboard the Mayflower and Elder Brewster guided them in a day of worship to God. William Bradford recorded their praise. "Being thus arrived in a good harbor and brought safe to land, they fell upon their knees and blessed the God of Heaven who had brought them over the vast and furious ocean."

Crossing Cape Cod Bay, the Pilgrims found Plymouth Rock and decided they would make their settlement there. They continued to live and sleep on board the Mayflower while they began construction on their new little community. The winter was harsh and about half of the new Americans died, including Bradford's wife, who fell off the ship and drowned. Disease, illness, and the cold took the rest.

Those that made it through the winter put their hearts, minds, and souls into their new world. In the spring of 1621, the Mayflower left to return to England and the Pilgrims met Native American Squanto. Squanto befriended the Englishmen teaching them how to fertilized the land, plant crops and fish. Bradford believed Squanto was a "special instrument sent of God for their good beyond their expectation." Squanto, along with his Indian brethren, were loved and admired by the Pilgrims. But as much as Squanto taught them, he couldn't make the crops grow because he couldn't make it rain.

In July of 1623 Bradford wrote of a horrible drought that plagued the community for months. Crops were beginning to wither under the extremely dry situation. It was then the Pilgrims "set apart a solemn day of humiliation, to seek the Lord by humble and fervent prayer, in this great distress. And He was pleased to give them a gracious and speedy answer, both to their own and the Indians' admiration that lived amongst them."

However, today's textbooks claim the first Thanksgiving was a celebration of thanks to the Indians for helping bring a good harvest. All references of God are removed, yet it is hard to argue when the facts are presented. Bradford made it clear he and the Pilgrims thanked God for their blessings. Rain came "which did so apparently revive and quicken the decayed corn and other fruits, as was wonderful to see, and made the Indians astonished to behold. And afterwards the Lord sent them such seasonable showers, with interchange of fair warm weather as, through His blessing, caused a fruitful and liberal harvest, to their no small comfort and rejoicing. For which mercy, in time convenient, they also set apart a day of thanksgiving. . . ." Some scholars are trying to rewrite history claiming this was not a reference to the traditional "Thanksgiving Day", arguing there was a separate thanksgiving day praising the Indians. Historical documents prove otherwise. Indians were definitely invited guests to the 3-day celebration but there is no mistake God was still the guest of honor.

The Pilgrims came here for the freedom to worship God. They truly appreciated the help and generosity of the Indians, however their thankfulness for those helpers went to God. To do otherwise would go against their whole purpose of coming to America. Though we must try our best to witness to God's greatness, there will always be those that will refuse to see Him. But what is indisputable, once the facts are reviewed, is this country was started by Christian people who gave all glory and honor to God the Father and founded a republic on Judeo-Christian values.

Thanks be to GOD!

That's my 2 cents.

Love,
Mom

Thanksgiving Proclamation 1777

November 27, 2014

Dear Liberty,

On November 1, 1777, the Second Continental Congress produced the National Thanksgiving Day Proclamation. It set aside Thursday, December 8, 1777, as a day of "Solemn Thanksgiving and Praise". This document once again is overwhelming proof our Founding Fathers were men of great faith and that our beloved United States of America was build on a strong Christian heritage.

FORASMUCH as it is the indispensable Duty of all Men to adore the superintending Providence of Almighty God; to acknowledge with Gratitude their Obligation to him for benefits received, and to implore such farther Blessings as they stand in Need of; And it having pleased him in his abundant Mercy not only to continue to us the innumerable Bounties of his common Providence, but also to smile upon us in the Prosecution of a just and necessary War, for the Defence and Establishment of our unalienable Rights and Liberties; particularly in that he hath been pleased in so great a Measure to prosper the Means used for the Support of our Troops and to crown our Arms with most signal success:

It is therefore recommended to the legislative or executive powers of these United States, to set apart Thursday, the eighteenth Day of December next, for Solemn Thanksgiving and Praise; That with one Heart and one Voice the good People may express the grateful Feelings of their Hearts, and consecrate themselves to the Service of their Divine Benefactor; and that together with their sincere Acknowledgments and Offerings, they may join the penitent Confession of their manifold Sins, whereby they had forfeited every Favour, and their humble and earnest Supplication that it may please God, through the Merits of Jesus Christ, mercifully to forgive and blot them out of Remembrance; That it may please him graciously to afford his Blessing on the Governments of these States respectively, and prosper the public Council of the whole; to inspire our Commanders both by Land and Sea, and all under them, with that Wisdom and Fortitude which may render them fit Instruments, under the

Providence of Almighty God, to secure for these United States the greatest of all human blessings, Independence and Peace; That it may please him to prosper the Trade and Manufactures of the People and the Labour of the Husbandman, that our Land may yet yield its Increase; To take Schools and Seminaries of Education, so necessary for cultivating the Principles of true Liberty, Virtue and Piety, under his nurturing Hand, and to prosper the Means of Religion for the promotion and enlargement of that Kingdom which consisteth in Righteousness, Peace and Joy in the Holy Ghost.

And it is further recommended, that servile Labour, and such Recreation as, though at other Times innocent, may be unbecoming the Purpose of this Appointment, be omitted on so solemn an Occasion.

    That's my 2 cents.

Love,
Mom

Yes, Liberty, There Is A Santa Claus

December 6, 2014

Dear Liberty,

In 325 AD, a priest named Arius was gaining followers and considerable support with his claim that Christ was created and not equal to God. Arianism flatly denied that Christ was present during creation and it brought into question the existence of a triune God. Arius made his argument at Nicaea after Emperor Constantine called together a council of Christian leaders to form a doctrine of unity within the church. As Arius made his argument, the Bishop of Myra quickly put Arius in his place by simply quoting one line of scripture, "In the beginning was the Word, and the Word was with God, and the Word was God." (John 1:1) And with that, the Bishop of Myra, also known as Jolly O' Saint Nick, punched Arius out. Nicholas' strong efforts in defending the faith, along with other church leaders, led to what is known as the Nicene Creed, a statement of faith repeated in churches to this very day. St. Methodius stated, "thanks to the teaching of St. Nicholas the metropolis of Myra alone was untouched by the filth of the Arian heresy, which it firmly rejected as death-dealing poison."

This, my dear Liberty, is the true Santa Claus. He is not a marketing gimmick to turn our attention away from Christ and his birth, but rather a defender of the faith and voice in the wilderness calling people back to God. As Christmas nears and talk begins of Black Friday sales and images of reindeer and a white bearded man in red selling Coca Cola make their rounds, perhaps it's good to go back and learn the truth of who St. Nicholas really was.

Almost 300 years after Christ, in the ancient city of Patara, located in modern-day Turkey, a baby boy was born to a wealthy Christian couple. They named him Nicholas and brought him up in the faith. While he was young, an epidemic swept the country and took the lives of his parents. He was taken in by his Uncle Nicholas, who was the Bishop of Patara, and raised in the church.

As a teenager, he traveled to the Holy Land, experiencing where Jesus lived, died and rose again. Legend tells that on his return trip to Patara a tremendous storm arose, threatening the safety of the ship and all aboard. Nicholas prayed for protection and the sea calmed, sparing the ship and all the lives onboard. Because of this act, Nicholas was declared the patron saint of sailors and voyagers.

Nicholas believed God called him to the ministry so he began his journey as a servant of the Lord. Over time he became a bishop and served the city of Myra, also in modern day Turkey. A fervent follower of Christ, he passionately spread the Gospel. This did not sit well with the Roman Emperor Diocletian, who in 303 AD directed the capture and torture of all Christians before throwing them in jail. Nicholas was arrested and imprisoned. He was severely beaten for his faith several times but never lost sight of his calling. While imprisoned he defended some other prisoners who were unjustly charged, adding to his legacy of humanity and justice. Once Emperor Constantine, the first Roman Emperor to embrace Christianity, assumed power in 306 AD, all Christian prisoners were released. Bishop Nicholas returned to Myra where he continued to profess the Good News of the Gospel.

As an only son, Nicholas was left with great wealth when his parents died. Following Jesus' command to serve others, he used his money to give gifts, food, and other necessities to the poor and needy. One such story was of a poor widowed man with three daughters who could not afford a proper dowry for even one daughter. If the young women were not properly married, they would more than likely end up as slaves. Nicholas secretly gave the man a dowry for each child. The legend holds that a bag of gold was thrown through a window, or down the chimney, landing in a stocking hanging from the mantel to dry. From this event the legend of St. Nicholas was born. When the father learned that Nicholas gave the dowries, Nicholas simply replied, "Don't thank me, thank God alone."

After his death on December 6, 343, Nicholas was given the title of Saint and the stories of his generosity, compassion and gift-giving only grew. His feast day is December 6th, known as St. Nicholas Day. In the 5th century nuns began anonymously depositing food baskets and clothes on the doorsteps of the needy on the night of December 6th in remembrance of St. Nicholas.

When Martin Luther and other reformers ushered in the Reformation in the mid-1500's, the worship of saints drastically died off. (see <u>The Knock Heard 'Round The World</u> and <u>Here I Stand</u>-Vol.4) However, St. Nicholas' life and legend not only continued but grew, taking on variations throughout the world. In Holland, St. Nicholas was referred to as "Sinterklaas". In Germany, Switzerland, and the Netherlands, shoes and stockings were left outside the door, hoping for some candy or treats from St. Nicholas. However, naughty boys and girls would wake to find only a lump of coal as their present.

Over time these stories and traditions were brought to America, modified and changed. Clement Clarke Moore wrote the poem <u>An Account of a Visit from St. Nicholas</u> in 1820, which made St. Nick a heavy, jolly man who slides down the chimney. Moore also gave St. Nick eight flying reindeer. In 1881, cartoonist Thomas Nast gave St. Nick the red suit with white fur trim, making St. Nick's transformation into Santa Claus complete.

As is common, most legends grow out of some bit of reality. Actual events are embellished and fantasized with variations in each story and tale but it is the grain of truth that is often the most remarkable. We do know there was a Saint Nicholas and that he was an incredibly faithful, God-fearing man who quite literally fought for the Gospel. He was even tortured and imprisoned for his beliefs, but refused to deny his Lord and Savior. He obeyed the words of Christ and used his wealth and good fortune to help the needy and poor. His legacy remains a map for each new generation that constantly points them to Jesus.

So yes, Liberty, there is a Santa Claus, and he was an amazing follower of Christ. So don't get distracted by the modern understanding of the jolly old man who gives you presents on Christmas. Focus instead on the bishop who risked his life and spent his family fortune professing and spreading the Good News of Jesus Christ. This is the Santa Claus you should remember. This is the Santa Claus you should emulate.

That's my 2 cents.

Love,
Mom

Glass Houses

December 12, 2014

Dear Liberty,

Earlier this week President Obama gave a speech trying to gather support for his unconstitutional actions of refusing to enforce laws regarding illegal immigrants. He quoted the Bible saying we should be kind to foreigners as we were once foreigners in this land ourselves. What he conveniently forgot to include were the passages that command there should be one set of laws for the native born as for the stranger.

"Native-born Israelites and foreigners are equal before the Lord and are subject to the same decrees. This is a permanent law for you, to be observed from generation to generation. The same instructions and regulations will apply both to you and to the foreigners living among you." (Numbers 15:15-16) This means that you cannot set separate legal standards for nationals verses immigrants.

Obama has conveniently overlooked that order from God and is granting special treatment to illegal aliens over America's own citizens. If I have to have a passport to lawfully enter this country after traveling outside it's boarders, then the same law applies to everyone. Those coming here without any documentation are breaking the law and should be refused entry, just as I would be if I did not have proper documentation. So while Obama is trying to shame Christians into bowing to his order, he himself is the one violating God's commands.

The Old Testament says we should not be cruel to, oppress, or take advantage of the aliens. "You must not mistreat or oppress foreigners in any way. Remember, you yourselves were once foreigners in the land of Egypt." (Exodus 22:21) However, the Democrats want poor immigrants here so they can make them a permanent oppressed voting underclass that is dependent on governmental handouts. Equally wrong are the GOP Republicans and rotary club activists that want them here to take advantage of their cheap labor. Both political agendas go completely against the scripture Obama is attempting to use to support his actions.

Ironically, in 2006 Senator Obama gave a speech claiming that people should not have to check their religion at the door, but they should also refrain from quoting scripture and using it as a basis for their argument so as not to offend people of other religions. President Obama apparently not only forgot that speech, he misused scripture trying to gain support for his actions and quite frankly infuriated those whose religion he was quoting! Thank you, Mr. President, but the American people are not the ones needing a religious lecture here.

Furthermore, Obama stated, "I think the good book says, 'don't throw stones in glass houses'." I'm assuming he is referring to the Bible. He might be referring to a Billy Joel album. The phrase does not come from the Bible. He was trying to make the point that we should not judge the illegals without looking at our own faults. I can only conclude he wants law-abiding citizens to forgive lawlessness because of the circumstances of the lawbreakers or he wants law-abiding citizens to decide following the law isn't worth it any more.

This is the same approach he has shown in Ferguson, Missouri, and in New York City. Pay no attention to a person's illegal actions. Instead look only at the color of their skin. Either way we are turning a country founded on laws into a cesspool of corruption and it is being done intentionally. What is even more egregious is that most immigrants coming to America are trying desperately to flee the criminality of their own countries while Obama openly embraces it.

To finish off this incredibly offensive speech, he uses the Christmas story to attempt to gather support for his lawlessness. He claims Mary and Joseph were foreigners in Bethlehem and could not find any place to stay when they arrived. Obama seemed to imply that because they were foreigners they were tossed in with the animals. Again, he could not be more inaccurate on his comparison.

Joseph was born in Bethlehem. He was far from a foreigner. He was returning home because a census was to be taken. Citizens had to return to their city of birth so as to register in person. Countless people were returning to Bethlehem at the same time and most stayed with relatives. Biblical scholars recently discovered that the word originally translated as "inn" could actually refer to the upper rooms of a house. Many now believe Joseph's relative's house was full so they had to stay in the lower room, which was occupied by the animals. They were not tossed aside because they were strangers in the city. God purposefully directed his Son, Our Lord and Savior, the King of Kings, to be born in the most humble way so as to completely and fully show his purpose on this earth. Not to rule the world, but to save it. For Obama to use this to try to gain sympathy for those breaking the law is unconscionable.

What he's doing is not rare. In fact Shakespeare revealed this very nature of evil in <u>The Merchant of Venice</u>. "The Devil can cite Scripture for his purpose. An evil soul producing holy witness is like a *villain with a smiling cheek, a goodly apple rotten at the heart." People with evil intent will often disguise themselves as angels of light.*

This merely follows in the slithering path of sin that Satan laid out for Adam and Eve. "Now the serpent was more crafty than any of the wild animals the Lord God had made. He said to the woman, "Did God really say, 'You must not eat from any tree in the garden'?" The woman said to the serpent, "We may eat fruit from the trees in the garden, but God did say, 'You must not eat fruit from the tree that is in the middle of the garden, and you must not touch it, or you will die.'" "You will not certainly die," the serpent said to the woman. "For God knows that when you eat from it your eyes will be opened, and you will be like God, knowing good and evil." (Gen 3:1-5)

All too often scripture, or attempts at scripture from the Book of Joel, will be used to mislead. Therefore continually read the scriptures like those at the Church at Berea did in the book of Acts. When Paul shared the Gospel of the Lord they "received the word with all readiness of mind, and searched the scriptures daily, whether those things were so."

Liberty, there are many across this nation who will probably have no idea how inaccurate and offensive Obama's statements are. Sadder still is how many won't even care. This would not have been the case 50, 30, even 20 years ago, but because of the incredible push of the progressives to replace God with government, too many are ignorant of this complete slap in the face of Bible believers.

It is at times like these that powerful people grab as much liberty and freedom from the people as they can. Your father and I will continue to fight to keep your inalienable rights intact. However, you must carry on the fight for liberty to pass it on to the next generation. This evil will not go away and you must continue to inform and educate everyone you can of the possible enslavement that is constantly threatening our freedom. As Ronald Reagan said, "Freedom is never more than one generation away from extinction. We didn't pass it to our children in the bloodstream. It must be fought for, protected, and handed on for them to do the same, or one day we will spend our sunset years telling our children and our children's children what it was once like in the United States where men were free."

God is very clear about those who misuse His Word. "I will forget you completely. I will expel you from my presence, along with this city that I gave to you and your ancestors. And I will make you an object of ridicule, and your name will be infamous throughout the ages." (Jeremiah 23:39-40) Obama is doing this at his own peril. Liberty, it is your responsibility to know the scriptures yourself and not be fooled or misled by anyone trying to twist God's Word for their own purpose.

That's my 2 cents.

Love,
Mom

I Believe I Can Fly

December 17, 2014

Dear Liberty,

As I explained in my very first letter to you (<u>Is Consensus Always Right?</u>), the Wright Brothers were not the only ones working on flight at the turn of the 20th Century. However, it was because of their tireless efforts that they realized that the universally accepted data on lift was inaccurate and had been for 150 years. After making the proper adjustments, the Wright Brothers designed and built several gliders, which they made trial run after trial run in a Dayton, Ohio field.

The truly remarkable aspect of this story is that neither of these men received a high school diploma, though Wilber was just shy of completing four years, let alone any higher education. Orville dropped out his junior year to start his own business. He designed and built, with Wilber's help, a printing press and they began publishing their own weekly newspaper. After a short time the brothers took advantage of the new bicycle trend, running a repair and service shop. Not long after, they started producing their own bicycle brand out of their store, Wright Cycle Company. It is out of this shop that the brothers brought flight to life.

Not having the winds needed for lift in Dayton, the brothers began exploring other areas of the country for a more suitable testing site, which they found in Kitty Hawk, North Carolina. The brothers disassembled their gliders, packed them up, and headed south. They spent two years testing gliders, perfecting wing control, or the three-axis control system, before deciding they had the proper aircraft ready. It was time to add power.

In 1903 their glider became a flyer. They headed to North Caroline once again for weeks of more tests, more obstructions and more frustrations. They were delayed for weeks due to broken engine shafts, which required two trips back to Dayton to make repairs. Blessed with perfect weather, they were ready to try a flight attempt on December 13, 1903. Being it was a Sunday though, the brothers, sons of a bishop in the church, put their reverence to God above their personal goals and rested on that day. On Monday morning they were ready to go with Wilbur winning the coin toss to be the first pilot. He made a 3-second flight but caused major damage to the flyer due to the aircraft stalling after takeoff. The flyer was repaired and the brothers were ready again on December 17, 1903. Orville was at the controls this time and he made the first successful flight of a self-propelled aircraft traveling 120 feet at a 10 feet altitude. Three more flights were made that day of 175 and 200 feet by Wilber and Orville respectfully and an amazing 852 feet by Wilber for the last flight of the day. The world would never be the same.

Less than 66 years later American innovators, both private and at NASA, took us to the moon! This is an unbelievable accomplishment. From America's efforts with space travel we have computers, Velcro, microwaves, Kidney dialysis machines, disposable diapers, satellite dishes, fire-resistant fabrics, and the internet, just to name a few.

Unfortunately, America has even begun to turn it's back on space travel. Under the keen eye of the Obama Administration, while the rest of the world continues to see the limitlessness of the universe, NASA's focus has become Muslim relations. Instead of inventing things like smoke detectors and fiber optics, America now works to become friends with people who enslave teenage women with the blessing of their holy book, the Quran, and blow up innocent children in schools in the name of Allah.

Others in the country are actually trying to deny the moon landings altogether. The thought is if you take away the great things America has achieved, you take away the greatness of America.

Liberty, you don't have to have a college degree to be successful. You don't have to have money to pursue your dreams. But most importantly you don't have to change your values and beliefs to satisfy academia to accomplish your goals. It is when people break from the chains of the status quo that they accomplish feats beyond their wildest imagination. Don't believe those who tell you that you cannot reach for the sky. Such people are too scared to reach themselves, or they are trying to control you. Either way, as long as you are not defying God's love and instruction for you, then nothing should stand in your way.

So on this day, we tip our hats to two bicycle makers who believed they could fly. Not only were they right, their vision changed the world.

That's my 2 cents.

Love,
Mom

The Reason for the Season

December 25, 2014

Dear Liberty,

In the sixth month of Elizabeth's pregnancy (with John the Baptist), God sent the angel Gabriel to Nazareth, a town in Galilee, to a virgin pledged to be married to a man named Joseph, a descendant of David. The virgin's name was Mary. The angel went to her and said, "Greetings, you who are highly favored! The Lord is with you."

Mary was greatly troubled at his words and wondered what kind of greeting this might be. But the angel said to her, "Do not be afraid, Mary; you have found favor with God. You will conceive and give birth to a son, and you are to call him Jesus. He will be great and will be called the Son of the Most High. The Lord God will give him the throne of his father David, and he will reign over Jacob's descendants forever; his kingdom will never end."

"How will this be," Mary asked the angel, "since I am a virgin?"

The angel answered, "The Holy Spirit will come on you, and the power of the Most High will overshadow you. So the holy one to be born will be called the Son of God. Even Elizabeth your relative is going to have a child in her old age, and she who was said to be unable to conceive is in her sixth month. For no word from God will ever fail."

"I am the Lord's servant," Mary answered. "May your word to me be fulfilled." Then the angel left her.

Mary was pledged to be married to Joseph, but before they came together, she was found to be pregnant through the Holy Spirit. Because Joseph her husband was faithful to the law, and yet did not want to expose her to public disgrace, he had in mind to divorce her quietly.

But after he had considered this, an angel of the Lord appeared to him in a dream and said, "Joseph son of David, do not be afraid to take Mary home as your wife, because what is conceived in her is from the Holy Spirit. She will give birth to a son, and you are to give him the name Jesus because he will save his people from their sins."

All this took place to fulfill what the Lord had said through the prophet: "The virgin will conceive and give birth to a son, and they will call him Immanuel" (which means "God with us").

When Joseph woke up, he did what the angel of the Lord had commanded him and took Mary home as his wife. But he did not consummate their marriage until she gave birth to a son.

In those days Caesar Augustus issued a decree that a census should be taken of the entire Roman world. (This was the first census that took place while Quirinius was governor of Syria.) And everyone went to their own town to register.

So Joseph also went up from the town of Nazareth in Galilee to Judea, to Bethlehem the town of David, because he belonged to the house and line of David. He went there to register with Mary, who was pledged to be married to him and was expecting a child. While they were there, the time came for the baby to be born, and she gave birth to her firstborn, a son. She wrapped him in cloths and placed him in a manger, because there was no guest room available for them.

And there were shepherds living out in the fields nearby, keeping watch over their flocks at night. An angel of the Lord appeared to them, and the glory of the Lord shone around them, and they were terrified. But the angel said to them, "Do not be afraid. I bring you good news that will cause great joy for all the people. Today in the town of David a Savior has been born to you; he is the Messiah, the Lord. This will be a sign to you: You will find a baby wrapped in cloths and lying in a manger."

Suddenly a great company of the heavenly host appeared with the angel, praising God and saying,
"Glory to God in the highest heaven,
and on earth peace to those on whom his favor rests."

When the angels had left them and gone into heaven, the shepherds said to one another, "Let's go to Bethlehem and see this thing that has happened, which the Lord has told us about."

So they hurried off and found Mary and Joseph, and the baby, who was lying in the manger. When they had seen him, they spread the word concerning what had been told them about this child, and all who heard it were amazed at what the shepherds said to them. But Mary treasured up all these things and pondered them in her heart. The shepherds returned, glorifying and praising God for all the things they had heard and seen, which were just as they had been told.

On the eighth day, when it was time to circumcise the child, he was named Jesus, the name the angel had given him before he was conceived.

(Excerpts from Matthew and Luke in NIV)

That's my 2 cents.

Love,
Mom

Liberating Letters — 2¢

"If freedom of speech is taken away, then dumb and silent we many be led, like sheep to the slaughter."
George Washington

TheFactsPaper.com

Liberating Letters — 2¢

"No people will tamely surrender their Liberties, nor can any be easily subdued, when knowledge is diffused and virtue is preserved. On the contrary, when people are universally ignorant, and debauched in their manners, they will sink under their own weight without the aid of foreign Invaders."
Samuel Adams
Founding Father and Signer of the Declaration of Independence

TheFactsPaper.com

Liberating Letters — 2¢

"My God! How little do my countrymen know what precious blessings they are in possession of, and which no other people on earth enjoy!"
Thomas Jefferson

TheFactsPaper.com

2¢ — "My only hope of salvation is in the infinite, transcendent love of God, manifested in the world by the death of His Son upon the cross. Nothing but His blood will wash away my sins. I relay exclusively upon it. Come, Lord Jesus! Come quickly!"

Dr. Benjamin Rush
Father of American Medicine
Signer of Declaration of Independence

LiberatingLetters
TheFactsPaper.com

Liberating Letters — **2¢**

The only thing necessary for the triumph of evil is for good men to do nothing.

Edmund Burke

TheFactsPaper.com

LiberatingLetters — **2¢**

"Back in the thirties we were told we must collectivize the nation because the people were so poor. Now we are told we must collectivize the nation because the people are so rich."

William F. Buckley

TheFactsPaper.com

Liberating Letters — 2¢

"You can always count on Americans to do the right thing - after they've tried everything else."

Winston Churchill

TheFactsPaper.com

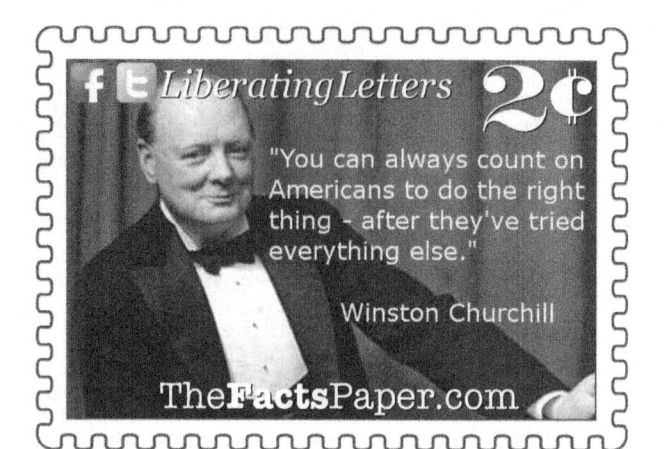

Liberating Letters — 2¢

Let each citizen remember at the moment he is offering his vote that he is not making a present or a compliment to please an individual - or at least that he ought not so to do; but that he is executing one of the most solemn trusts in human society for which he is accountable to God and his country."
Samuel Adams

TheFactsPaper.com

Pictures

*All Flickr photos are used under the terms of the following license:
https://creativecommons.org/licenses/by/2.0/legalcode

Change The World
    NASA Blue Marble 2007 West –
    By: NASA Goddard Space Flight Center @ Flicker

    NASA Blue Marble 2007 East –
    By: NASA Goddard Space Flight Center @ Flicker

Hear No Evil, Speak No Evil?:
    speak no evil - By: Emilio Küffer @ Flicker

The Real Hunger Games
    Baked my first loaf of bread! - By: Mack Male @ Flicker

Father's Day
    Father and son handshake - By: Alex Krasavtsev @ Flicker

Sleeping Beauty
    Reese Napping - By: Donnie Ray Jones @ Flicker

Is Justice Blind?
    Golden Lady Justice, Bruges, Belgium -
    By: Emmanuel Huybrechts @ Flicker

Keeping the Faith
    Holy Bible – By: Steve Snodgrass @ Flicker
    (Edited photo by deleting background)

Thanks Be To God
    First Fun Thanksgiving, after J.L.G. Ferris -
    By: Mike Licht @ Flicker

Glass Houses
    Broken Glass Shards Urban Exploration April 19, 2010 –
    By: Steven Depolo @ Flicker

The Reason For The Season
    Nativity – By: Jeff Weese @ Flicker

References

Is Consensus Always Right?
http://wrightstories.com/wright-brothers-get-a-lift/

"Soylent Green is made out of people!"
http://en.wikipedia.org/wiki/Moloch
http://www.imdb.com/title/tt0070723/plotsummary
http://en.wikipedia.org/wiki/Soylent_Green

The Sounds of a Revolution
http://www.history.com/topics/american-revolution/boston-tea-party
http://en.wikipedia.org/wiki/United_States_Declaration_of_Independence
http://www.history.com/news/10-things-you-may-not-know-about-the-boston-tea-party

Fruit of the Forbidden Tree
http://www.theblaze.com/stories/2014/04/29/did-i-just-say-that-emmy-award-winning-actress-opens-up-about-anguishing-experience-of-having-an-abortion/
http://en.wikipedia.org/wiki/Mao_Zedong
https://answers.yahoo.com/question/index?qid=20070524035053AALFG5b
https://answers.yahoo.com/question/index?qid=20100219111218AAcIHkh
http://www.holodomorct.org/history.html
https://answers.yahoo.com/question/index?qid=20070524042140AAkFM3K
http://www.independent.co.uk/arts-entertainment/books/news/maos-great-leap-forward-killed-45-million-in-four-years-2081630.html
https://answers.yahoo.com/question/index?qid=20081020235334AAdIkge

A Hero's Story
http://en.wikipedia.org/wiki/1st_Infantry_Division_%28United_States%29
http://www.huffingtonpost.com/jack-mirkinson/check-my-privilege-please_b_5281197.html
http://www.realclearpolitics.com/articles/2014/04/30/checking_my_privilege_character_as_the_basis_of_privilege_122473.html
http://www.glennbeck.com/2014/05/08/white-guys-we-suck-and-were-sorry-glenn-reacts-to-bizarre-new-video-that-apologizes-for-years-of-white-privilege/

Hear No Evil, Speak No Evil?
http://www.theguardian.com/world/2013/apr/01/greece-golden-dawn-global-ambitions
http://www.thenewamerican.com/usnews/politics/item/2455-obamas-friend-ayers-kill-25-million-americans
http://hnn.us/article/1796
http://legalinsurrection.com/2014/05/just-when-you-thought-the-white-privilege-conference-could-not-get-any-worse/

Memorial Day - Honoring the Highest Sacrifice
http://denyyourselfdaily.blogspot.com/2008/03/george-washingtons-prayer.html

The Real Hunger Game

http://www.theblaze.com/stories/2014/05/24/six-absolutely-stunning-details-from-suspected-santa-barbara-shooters-141-page-manifesto/
http://en.wikipedia.org/wiki/List_of_school_shootings_in_the_United_States

D-Day vs. Today - How Far We've Come
http://www.glennbeck.com/2014/06/06/remarkable-audio-fdr-leads-nation-in-poignant-prayer-in-d-day-radio-address/
http://www.theguardian.com/world/2009/sep/05/chamberlain-munich-appeasement-second-world-war
http://yappi.com/forums/showthread.php?t=266472

Father's Day
http://www.womeninthescriptures.com/2010/11/real-meaning-of-term-help-meet.html
http://blog.cbeinternational.org/2006/11/does-it-really-mean-helpmate/

Sleeping Beauty
http://en.wikipedia.org/wiki/Tooth
http://health.howstuffworks.com/human-body/systems/digestive/question464.htm
http://en.wikipedia.org/wiki/Monotreme
https://answersingenesis.org/evidence-against-evolution/probability/does-evolution-have-a-chance/
http://www.freerepublic.com/focus/f-bloggers/1435562/posts

The Candy Bomber
http://en.wikipedia.org/wiki/End_of_World_War_II_in_Europe
http://en.wikipedia.org/wiki/Berlin_Blockade
http://www.trumanlibrary.org/teacher/berlin.htm
http://www.charlesbridge.com/productdetails.cfm?PC=5346
http://en.wikipedia.org/wiki/Soviet_Union_in_World_War_II
http://militaryhistory.about.com/od/aerialcampaigns/p/berlinairlift.htm
http://www.capmembers.com/media/cms/Uncle_Wiggly_Halvorsen_Story_LR_E5143D25300A3.pdf
http://en.wikipedia.org/wiki/Allied-occupied_Germany
http://blog-stampofapproval.com/tag/berlin-airlift/

The Birth of a Movement
http://en.wikipedia.org/wiki/Charles_Sumner
http://en.wikipedia.org/wiki/Kansas-Nebraska_Act
http://en.wikipedia.org/wiki/Bleeding_Kansas
http://en.wikipedia.org/wiki/Slave_Power
http://www.ushistory.org/us/31e.asp
http://www.senate.gov/artandhistory/history/minute/The_Caning_of_Senator_Charles_Sumner.htm
http://brownvboard.org/content/prelude-brown-1849-roberts-v-city-boston

Happy Independence Day
http://en.wikipedia.org/wiki/Signing_the_United_States_Declaration_of_Independence
http://en.wikipedia.org/wiki/Jefferson_Bible
http://www.beliefnet.com/News/2005/02/The-Peoples-Bible-Goes-To-Washington.aspx#
http://wrenncom.com/CommentaryArchives/2001/20y01m07d04-01.asp

Man on the Moon
http://buzzaldrin.com/the-man/biography/
http://www.snopes.com/glurge/communion.asp
http://www.truthorfiction.com/rumors/a/aldrin-communion.htm#.U8iARKjKkcs
http://en.wikipedia.org/wiki/Buzz_Aldrin
http://en.wikipedia.org/wiki/Neil_Armstrong
http://history1900s.about.com/od/1960s/a/jfkmoon.htm
http://www.glendorachurch.com/articles/2009/07-18-09.htm

Is History Repeating Again?
http://www.glennbeck.com/2014/08/04/is-there-anyone-else-in-the-media-who-will-join-me-glenn-reacts-to-nancy-pelosis-bold-break-of-protocol/
http://www.washingtonpost.com/politics/sen-ted-cruz-of-texas-is-a-rising-republican-power-in-house-as-well-as-a-whip/2014/07/31/10e5a87a-18ed-11e4-85b6-c1451e622637_story.html
http://www.politico.com/story/2014/08/tom-marino-nancy-pelosi-fight-109685.html
http://abcnews.go.com/blogs/politics/2014/08/pelosi-chases-republican-tom-marino-across-house-chamber/

Just The Facts, Ma'am
http://www.ijreview.com/2014/08/169517-report-officer-involved-ferguson-shooting-suffered-orbital-blowout-fracture-eye-socket/
http://www.theblaze.com/stories/2014/08/18/report-more-than-a-dozen-witnesses-have-corroborated-officer-darren-wilsons-version-of-ferguson-shooting/
http://www.theblaze.com/stories/2014/08/18/cnn-now-reporting-potential-bombshell-in-ferguson-shooting-regarding-what-alleged-friend-of-officer-darren-wilson-told-theblazes-dana-loesch-on-air/

Family Feud
http://www.inplainsite.org/html/isaac_ishmael.html
http://en.wikipedia.org/wiki/Ishmael_in_Islam
http://www.answering-islam.org/Shamoun/sacrifice.htm
http://www.judaism-islam.com/was-abraham-commanded-to-sacrifice-isaac-or-ishmael/
https://www.christiancourier.com/articles/1161-ishmael-or-isaac-the-koran-or-the-bible
http://therefinersfire.org/ishmael_and_isaac.htm
http://www.religionconflictpeace.org/volume-2-issue-2-spring-2009/isaac-and-ishmael
http://www.assistnews.net/Stories/2005/s05040110.htm
http://en.wikipedia.org/wiki/Israeli_Declaration_of_Independence http://patriotsforisrael.com/israelistatehood.htm
http://watchmanbiblestudy.com/Articles/1948PropheciesFulfilled.htm
http://en.wikipedia.org/wiki/Israeli–Palestinian_conflict
http://en.wikipedia.org/wiki/History_of_Islam
http://bibletranslation.ws/birth-of-islam/
http://festivals.awesomeji.com/barah-wafat/birth-of-islam.html
http://www.metmuseum.org/toah/hd/isla/hd_isla.htm
http://www.biblereferenceguide.com/keywords/ishmael.html
http://www.breitbart.com/Breitbart-TV/2014/07/13/Netanyahu-We-Use-

Missile-Defense-to-Protect-Our-People-They-Use-People-To-Protect-Their-Missiles
http://en.wikipedia.org/wiki/Mecca
http://www.religionfacts.com/islam/places/mecca.htm
http://en.wikipedia.org/wiki/Kaaba
https://answers.yahoo.com/question/index?qid=20090914092956AAEkO6z
http://www.religionfacts.com/islam/fastfacts.htm
http://www.religionfacts.com/islam/comparison_charts/islamic_sects.htm
http://en.wikipedia.org/wiki/Desert_of_Paran
http://en.wikipedia.org/wiki/Beersheba
http://studygrowknowblog.com/2013/06/18/did-abraham-or-ishmael-ever-go-to-mecca/
http://www.evidenceforchristianity.org/where-and-when-did-islam-originate-did-ishmael-son-of-abraham-start-this-religion/
http://www.vanguardngr.com/2013/09/abraham-ishmael-and-kaaba/
https://answers.yahoo.com/question/index?qid=20140212203032AALmKLv
http://en.wikipedia.org/wiki/History_of_Jerusalem
http://en.wikipedia.org/wiki/Temple_Mount
https://answers.yahoo.com/question/index?qid=20140731085747AAqOMFB

The Man Who Refused To Be King
http://en.wikipedia.org/wiki/Lucius_Quinctius_Cincinnatus
http://ancienthistory.about.com/od/rulersleaderskings/p/Cincinnatus.htm
http://www.mountvernon.org/research-collections/digital-encyclopedia/article/cincinnatus/
http://www.cato.org/publications/commentary/man-who-would-not-be-king
http://www.mountvernon.org/research-collections/digital-encyclopedia/article/constitutional-convention/
http://www.archives.gov/exhibits/charters/constitution_founding_fathers_virginia.html
http://www.therealamericanhis-story.com/gw
http://en.wikipedia.org/wiki/Society_of_the_Cincinnati
http://www.schillerinstitute.org/fid_02-06/2006/061_2-3_poe_purloined.html

Never Forget
http://cnsnews.com/news/article/brittany-m-hughes/kerry-real-face-islam-peaceful-religion
http://www.breitbart.com/Breitbart-TV/2014/09/03/Kerry-The-Bible-Commands-America-Protects-The-Planet-For-Muslim-Countries
http://lastresistance.com/7182/al-gore-flashback-2007-arctic-ice-will-completely-gone-seven-years/
http://www.kenmore.org/ferryfarm/boyhood.html
http://www.biography.com/people/john-quincy-adams-9175983#younger-years
http://www.history.com/topics/9-11-timeline
http://en.wikipedia.org/wiki/World_Trade_Center
http://en.wikipedia.org/wiki/Hijackers_in_the_September_11_attacks
http://www.fairus.org/issue/identity-and-immigration-status-of-9-11-terrorists
http://en.wikipedia.org/wiki/Takbir
http://news.investors.com/ibd-editorials/010511-558932-the-meaning-of-allah-akbar.htm
http://en.wikipedia.org/wiki/Casualties_of_the_September_11_attacks

We Reserve The Right To Refuse Service
http://www.christianpost.com/news/did-jesus-say-anything-about-homosexuality-120501/
http://illinoisfamily.org/homosexuality/homosexual-activist-admits-true-purpose-of-battle-is-to-destroy-marriage/
http://wbmoore.wordpress.com/2008/07/30/christ-did-speak-out-against-homosexuality/
http://www.theblaze.com/stories/2013/04/29/lesbian-activists-surprisingly-candid-speech-gay-marriage-fight-is-a-lie-to-destroy-marriage/

Is Justice Blind?
http://www.historynet.com/today-in-history
http://en.m.wikipedia.org/wiki/Judiciary_Act_of_1789
http://www.fjc.gov/history/home.nsf/page/landmark_02.html
http://www.answers.com/Q/What_was_the_Judiciary_Act_of_1789_and_why_was_it_important
http://en.m.wikipedia.org/wiki/Judicial_Procedures_Reform_Bill_of_1937
http://en.m.wikipedia.org/wiki/United_States_circuit_court
http://en.m.wikipedia.org/wiki/United_States_district_court
http://www.rushlimbaugh.com/daily/2008/10/28/barack_obama_s_anti_bill_of_rights
http://cnsnews.com/news/article/kagan-sits-judgment-obamacare-despite-cheering-its-passage-and-assigning-lawyer-defend
http://en.wikipedia.org/wiki/Harriet_Miers_Supreme_Court_nomination
http://www.usconstitution.org/federal-judiciary/details/circuit-judges-act-of-1869-16-stat-44-1869
http://www.constitution.org/uslaw/judiciary_1789.htm

Actions Speak Louder Than Words
http://7online.com/politics/major-rally-focusing-on-climate-change-taking-place-sunday-in-nyc/317693/
http://nypost.com/2014/09/22/climate-change-skeptics-call-out-marchers-hypocrisies/
http://askmarion.wordpress.com/2010/10/03/quick-one-nation-rally-vs-restore-honor-rally-comparison-updated/
http://www.breitbart.com/Big-Government/2014/09/29/NYC-Climate-March
http://www.technologyreview.com/news/516711/why-toyota-and-gm-are-pushing-fuel-cell-cars-to-market/
http://www.factcheck.org/2011/10/obamas-solyndra-problem/
http://www.gallup.com/poll/1576/abortion.aspx
http://en.wikipedia.org/wiki/Reactions_to_the_Deepwater_Horizon_oil_spill
http://money.cnn.com/2012/10/22/news/economy/obama-energy-bankruptcies/
http://www.nationalreview.com/article/388787/should-we-hope-die-75-victor-davis-hanson
http://www.dailymail.co.uk/news/article-2765461/Robert-F-Kennedy-Jr-loses-cool-grabs-mic-reporter-pushing-carbon-footprint.html

What is Columbus Day?
http://www.bbc.co.uk/schools/primaryhistory/famouspeople/christopher_columbus/
http://www.britannica.com/EBchecked/topic/127070/Christopher-Columbus
http://www.catholiceducation.org/articles/history/world/wh0024.html

http://www.history.com/topics/exploration/christopher-columbus
http://en.wikipedia.org/wiki/Christopher_Columbus
http://blogs.scientificamerican.com/cross-check/2010/11/22/thanksgiving-guilt-trip-how-warlike-were-native-americans-before-europeans-showed-up/
http://en.wikipedia.org/wiki/Trail_of_Tears

Keeping The Faith
http://hushmoney.org/501c3-facts.htm
http://blog.speakupmovement.org/church/churches-and-politics/bill-introduced-to-repeal-the-johnson-amendment/
http://www.thepowerhour.com/news2/lbj_churches.htm
http://politicaloutcast.com/2014/10/houston-officials-demanding-churches-turn-over-sermons/
http://www.wnd.com/2014/10/major-u-s-city-demands-oversight-of-sermons/
http://www.wallbuilders.com/libissuesarticles.asp?id=123
http://freedomoutpost.com/2014/10/houston-queer-mayor-stands-subpoena-lawlessness-gets-national-exposure/

Love The One You're With
http://www.caintv.com/uk-woman-i-wish-id-aborted-my
http://www.dailymail.co.uk/femail/article-2803834/I-wish-d-aborted-son-ve-spent-47-years-caring-s-shocking-admission-read-judge.html

The Knock Heard 'Round The World
http://www.prca.org/books/portraits/luther.htm
http://en.wikipedia.org/wiki/Martin_Luther
http://www.susanlynnpeterson.com/luther/reform.html
http://www.luther.de/en/ws.html
http://catholiceducation.org/articles/history/world/wh0075.html
http://catholiceducation.org/articles/history/world/wh0055.html
http://www.economist.com/node/21541719
http://www.bbc.co.uk/history/british/tudors/english_reformation_01.shtml
http://www.britannica.com/EBchecked/topic/495422/Reformation
http://www.britannica.com/EBchecked/topic/351950/Martin-Luther
https://answers.yahoo.com/question/index?qid=20071015072420AA2RZM4
http://www.history.com/topics/crusades
http://www.luther.de/en/95thesen.html
http://www.theblaze.com/stories/2014/11/02/how-a-sign-from-god-led-to-a-revolution-and-a-reformation-that-forever-transformed-the-christian-faith/

The Truth Shall Set You Free
http://www.patheos.com/blogs/warrenthrockmorton/2013/01/17/was-the-national-rifle-association-started-to-drive-out-the-kkk/
http://www.theblaze.com/stories/2013/01/16/nrthings-you-never-knew-about-the-second-amendment/
http://www.academia.org/progressive-segregation/
http://egnorance.blogspot.com/2012/10/segregation-was-liberal-policy.html
http://en.wikipedia.org/wiki/Declaration_of_war_by_the_United_States
http://en.wikipedia.org/wiki/Woodrow_Wilson
http://en.wikipedia.org/wiki/Racial_segregation_in_the_United_States
http://www.pbs.org/wnet/jimcrow/stories_events_segregation.html
http://www.pbs.org/wnet/jimcrow/stories_events_14th.html
http://law2.umkc.edu/faculty/projects/ftrials/conlaw/thirteenthamendment.h

tml
http://history.howstuffworks.com/history-vs-myth/japanese-internment-camp.htm
http://history.howstuffworks.com/history-vs-myth/japanese-internment-camp1.htm
http://history.howstuffworks.com/history-vs-myth/japanese-internment-camp2.htm
http://history.howstuffworks.com/history-vs-myth/japanese-internment-camp3.htm
http://en.wikipedia.org/wiki/Robert_Byrd
http://www.dianedew.com/sanger.htm
https://www.lifesitenews.com/news/how-planned-parenthood-targets-blacks-and-hispanics-new-interactive-online
http://www.glennbeck.com/2014/10/23/van-jones-tells-dana-loesch-yeah-palin-had-us-shaking-in-our-boots-in-08/
http://en.wikipedia.org/wiki/Condoleezza_Rice

Happy Veterans Day
http://www.va.gov/opa/vetsday/vetdayhistory.asp
http://en.wikipedia.org/wiki/Veterans_Day
http://en.wikipedia.org/wiki/Armistice_Day
http://www.history.com/topics/holidays/veterans-day-facts
https://www.dosomething.org/blog/11-facts-about-veterans-day
http://www.brainyquote.com/quotes/keywords/veterans.html
http://www2.dsu.nodak.edu/users/dmeier/Holocaust/hitler.html
http://en.wikipedia.org/wiki/World_War_I
http://en.wikipedia.org/wiki/Allies_of_World_War_I
http://en.wikipedia.org/wiki/Central_Powers
http://en.wikipedia.org/wiki/Treaty_of_Versailles
http://en.wikipedia.org/wiki/Assassination_of_Archduke_Franz_Ferdinand_of_Austria
http://www.firstworldwar.com/bio/ferdinand.htm
http://www.britannica.com/EBchecked/topic/323626/Kristallnacht

A Tale Of Two Women
http://www.thecurestartsnow.org/heroes/163/
http://www.cincinnati.com/story/sports/columnists/john-erardi/2014/11/08/erardi-lauren-hill-tells-uc-crowd-she-cant-believe-support/18700033/
http://www.usatoday.com/story/sports/ncaaw/2014/10/26/womens-basketball-lauren-hill-cancer-life-lessons/17959745/
http://www.glennbeck.com/2014/11/06/watch-lauren-hill-shares-the-incredible-story-of-her-battle-against-brain-cancer/
http://www.local12.com/news/features/top-stories/stories/one-last-game-18984.shtml
http://www.nydailynews.com/life-style/health/compassion-cares-busy-week-maynard-death-article-1.2007288
http://www.fox19.com/story/26732725/oregon-woman-wants-to-die-with-dignity
http://www.christianpost.com/news/one-life-lost-all-lives-diminished-brittany-maynard-and-assisted-suicide-129445/

Thanks Be To God!
http://americanhistory.about.com/od/holidays/a/thanksgiving_ff.htm

http://www.ushistory.org/us/3b.asp
http://www.pilgrimhallmuseum.org/pdf/TG_What_Happened_in_1621.pdf
http://education-portal.com/academy/lesson/governor-william-bradford-writings-role-in-the-first-thanksgiving.html#lesson
http://www.rushlimbaugh.com/daily/2011/11/23/the_real_story_of_thanksgiving
http://www.rushlimbaugh.com/daily/2004/11/24/george_washington_s_first_thanksgiving_proclamation_1789
http://www.heritage.org/initiatives/first-principles/primary-sources/washingtons-thanksgiving-proclamation
http://mayflowerhistory.com/bradford-william/
http://www.pilgrimhallmuseum.org/william_bradford.htm
http://www.pilgrimhallmuseum.org/pdf/Bradford_Passage_Starving_Time.pdf
http://www.pilgrimhallmuseum.org/pdf/Bradford_Passage_Clarks_Island.pdf
http://www.pilgrimhallmuseum.org/mayflower_compact_text.htm
http://en.wikipedia.org/wiki/Johannes_Gutenberg
http://en.wikipedia.org/wiki/Printing_press
http://www.ctlibrary.com/ch/1990/issue28/2825.html
http://americanhistory.about.com/od/colonialamerica/a/may_compact.htm
http://en.wikipedia.org/wiki/Colony_of_Virginia
http://billofrightsinstitute.org/resources/educator-resources/americapedia/americapedia-documents/mayflower-compact/
http://biblescripture.net/Pilgrims.html
http://biblescripture.net/Thanksgiving.html
http://en.wikipedia.org/wiki/List_of_Mayflower_passengers_who_died_at_sea_November/December_1620
http://en.wikipedia.org/wiki/John_Howland
http://www.ifapray.org/archive/PrayerGuides/PilgrimPrayerAndFasting-AModelForToday.pdf

Yes, Liberty, There Is A Santa Claus
https://www.facebook.com/video.php?v=10152844393103735
http://en.wikipedia.org/wiki/Saint_Nicholas
http://www.biography.com/people/st-nicholas-204635#reputation
http://www.catholic.org/saints/saint.php?saint_id=371
http://www.stnicholascenter.org/pages/who-is-st-nicholas/
http://www.stnicholascenter.org/pages/real-person/
http://www.stnicholascenter.org/pages/real-saint/
http://www.stnicholascenter.org/pages/my-kind-of-santa/
http://www.stnicksday.com/
http://newadvent.org/cathen/11063b.htm
http://en.wikipedia.org/wiki/First_Council_of_Nicaea

Glass Houses
http://www.theblaze.com/stories/2014/12/10/obama-keeps-citing-the-bible-to-tout-immigration-reform-but-do-you-remember-what-he-said-about-doing-just-that-in-2006/
http://www.theblaze.com/stories/2014/12/10/there-appears-to-be-something-wrong-with-the-bible-verse-obama-cited-to-push-immigration-action/

I Believe I Can Fly
http://www.lindberghfoundation.org/docs/index.php/media-a-

resources/aviation-history-timeline
http://en.wikipedia.org/wiki/Wright_brothers
http://en.wikipedia.org/wiki/Wright_Flyer
http://www.wright-brothers.org/History_Wing/Wright_Story/Inventing_the_Airplane/December_17_1903/December_17_1903.htm

Made in the USA
Monee, IL
28 July 2020